The Big Three

Harsh Bhasin, a veteran diplomat with a career spanning over three-and-a-half decades in the Indian Foreign Service, served as Ambassador to Denmark, High Commissioner to South Africa and Botswana, and as Consul General in New York and Johannesburg. A major portion of his work as a career diplomat was in China—during the Cultural Revolution and later—and in the course of three different assignments in the US in the 1970s through the 1990s. This book owes its origins to the long years he has spent living and working intimately in both China and the US.

After retirement from India's diplomatic service he has served on the faculty of the State University of New York at Stony Brook, first as a Visiting Professor in the Department of Political Science and later in the Department of Asian and Asian-American Studies. He currently holds the position of Chair in the Department.

THE BIG THREE

The Emerging Relationship between
the United States, India and China
in the Changing World Order

HARSH BHASIN

ACADEMIC FOUNDATION

NEW DELHI

First published in 2009
by

ACADEMIC FOUNDATION
4772-73 / 23 Bharat Ram Road, (23 Ansari Road),
Darya Ganj, New Delhi - 110 002 (India).
Phones : 23245001 / 02 / 03 / 04.
Fax : +91-11-23245005.
E-mail : books@academicfoundation.com
www. academicfoundation.com

Cataloging in Publication Data--DK
   Courtesy: D.K. Agencies (P) Ltd. <docinfo@dkagencies.com>

Bhasin, Harsh.
   The big three : the emerging relationship between the United
States, India and China in the changing world order / Harsh Bhasin.
   p.   cm.
   ISBN 13: 9788171887279
   ISBN 10: 8171887279

   1. United States--Foreign relations--India. 2. India--Foreign
relations--United States. 3. India--Foreign relations--China.
4. China--Foreign relations--India. 5. United States--Foreign
relations--China. 6. China--Foreign relations--United States.
I. Title.

DDC 327.54   22

Typeset and designed by Italics India, New Delhi.
Printed and bound in India.

0 1 2 3 4 5 6 7 8 9

Contents

Author's Note

This is a story of three countries with which I have the deepest ties—through birth, education and my professional career.

The first, India, is the country that I was born in and which nurtured me through life, education and career took me to the other two. Of the remaining two, the United States is my home today and will be the home to future generations of my family. And the third, China, is a country that holds a special attraction—a country where I started my diplomatic career and then became 'home' for seven rewarding years and which I grew to admire and respect as much as the other two and then some.

For someone with an abiding interest in international affairs, it is entirely fortuitous that of these three countries, one is an established (some say sole) superpower, the other appears to be on the fast track to get there and the remaining one has great aspirations, as well as impeccable credentials, to become one.

It is between these three fascinating nations—each truly unique in its culture and outlook—that I have spent three quarters of my life as well as my working career. Little wonder, therefore, that I have been motivated enough to attempt this humble examination of half-a-century of their mutual inter-relationship—often inimical, sometimes friendly, but always interesting—mirroring in a sense their three different civilisational approaches to issues and problems in the rough and tumble of the international jungle.

What is undeniable is that in the past half-a-century each had a history of a troubled relationship with the other, which explains the sub-title of this book—*Dynamics of a wary Inter-relationship*—because at different times during the foregoing five decades any one of the three nations was among the causes of differences between the other two. The book will attempt to analyse the reasons and underlying causes for these differences as the three most populous and powerful nations strive to put those differences behind and chart a new relationship in the 21st century.

The treatment of the subject matter will, thus, closely follow the pattern outlined above, namely involving an examination of the past history, present challenges and the way ahead, between each pair of countries—India and US, India and China, and US and China—before arriving at some final conclusions in the last chapter.

Unlike, say, thermodynamics, whose firmly established laws never change, international relations is a field in a state of constant flux, with shifting alliances, changing priorities and worse; the only 'constant' is the one immortalised by Lord Palmerston in his famous 19th century dictum on international relations: "There are no permanent friends or permanent enemies, only permanent interests." Extrapolated into the India-US-China equation, indeed they have never been each other's permanent friend or permanent enemy but perhaps something in between, yet permanently interested in each other and, lately, increasingly conscious of their inter-relationship. Why? Because each in its own interest (the only 'permanent' factor) does not wish the other two to get too close for its own comfort. How this is playing out on the international stage is the essential subject matter of this book.

Despite its singular authorship, a work of this nature can never be the outcome of a single-handed effort. The list of all those who, directly or indirectly, helped me in this writing would be far too long to enumerate. Most significantly, my long years in the Indian Foreign Service provided me with the practical experience and relevant background in international affairs to attempt this venture, and the State University of New York at Stony Brook provided the remaining wherewithal—from a conducive academic atmosphere to excellent library and research facilities—to give concrete shape to the venture. I am, indeed, indebted beyond words to both the institutions for making this a reality. On a personal note, I would be remiss if I failed to record the constant encouragement and constructive criticism of my wife, Kumkum, (herself an author), son Aditya, daughter Madhuri and their families, throughout the writing. I would like to thank my student, Mitch Fourman, at Stony Brook, for his help in researching various topics, including the timelines.

Finally, this book is dedicated to my Indian-American grandchildren, Shreyas and Shivanjali, who will grow up in a world where they will find the United States increasingly involved with both India and China in shouldering the responsibility to shape a politically, economically and environmentally secure future for the world.

Taking recourse to some hackneyed phrases, let me just place on record that the views, projections, prognostications or conclusions in the ensuing pages are entirely my own, and do not, in any way reflect the views of the government that I proudly served in different diplomatic capacities for over three and a half decades, or indeed of the prestigious academic institution where I enjoy the unique privilege to serve today.

Harsh Bhasin

Department of Asian and Asian-American Studies
State University of New York
Stony Brook, New York, USA

Abbreviations

CCP	Chinese Communist Party
CENTO	Central Treaty Organisation
CTBT	Comprehensive Test Ban Treaty
FDI	Foreign Direct Investment
FII	Foreign Institutional Investment
HOG	Head of Government
HOS	Head of State
KMT	Kuo Min Tang (Nationalist Chinese Party)
LAC	Line of Actual Control
LOC	Line of Control
NAM	Non-Aligned Movement
NATO	North Atlantic Treaty Organisation
NPT/NNPT	Nuclear Non-Proliferation Treaty
NWS	Nuclear Weapon State
PLA	People's Liberation Army (China's Armed Forces)
PRC	People's Republic of China
ROC	Republic of China (Taiwan)
SEATO	South East Asia Treaty Organisation
USLO	United States Liaison Office (in Beijing 1972-1979)
WW	World War

Introduction

The evolving relationship between the US, India and China is generally regarded as the most important feature in the emerging international political landscape of the 21st century. The post-war dominance of the transatlantic alliance, rooted in the overwhelming political, military and economic might of the US led eventually to the collapse of the Soviet Union and the end of the Cold War towards the closing years of the 20th century. This was not quite the 'end of the world' as we knew it, but simply the rebirth of a new one—one in which the bipolar world order gave way to a unipolar one, and still led by the US. But then, the very forces that brought about an end to the Cold War also unleashed a new torrent of liberalisation that countries like China and India—the epithet-laden drowsy Dragon and the sleeping Elephant—were quick to take advantage of, only to emerge in the first few years of the 21st century as formidable players on the world stage, ready to challenge the might of the traditional post-war power structures—indeed including even the post-Cold War politico-economic order.

It is interesting to note how conveniently old shibboleths were discarded in this quest for a new world order. China, the mighty Communist monolith, embraced capitalism with uninhibited alacrity given the enormous economic and political benefits the new policies brought in their wake. India, the self-proclaimed champion of non-alignment in politics and Fabian socialism in economics quickly re-engineered both to seek close ties with the sole surviving superpower and open up its hitherto nearly-closed economy to unabashed foreign investment and trade, again for the same economic and political benefits that rival China had reaped, albeit with a decade's head start in the race.

For many years, both India and China ran the development race with their hands voluntarily tied to their ideological backs—in the first case due to an inherent distrust of any policy of liberal trade or foreign investment dating back to East India Company days, and in the second case due to an equally blind belief in the socialist economic theories of Marx and Lenin. Not until both dogmas were discarded by each nation in the name of pragmatism did the process of meaningful (as opposed to rhetorical) economic development and the process of poverty alleviation really begin. And once it did, both countries achieved unprecedented rates of economic growth, bringing along with it wealth and prestige, influence and power. China found her niche in manufacturing and cheap exports with which she has clasped the mightiest world economy in its tentacle-like grasp, of which the latter is becoming increasingly wary. A gentler India is trying to catch up fast, albeit using the softer approach through software development, becoming an outsourcing hub (both for business-processing as well as knowledge-processing operations) and an increasingly preferred venue by major multinationals for their back-office operations.

However, no matter which way you look at it, the US, India and China today cover between themselves some 40 per cent of the world's population, nearly half of all the world trade, and probably an even larger chunk of the global economy. That is reason enough for a serious study of their emerging inter-relationship. A deeper glance will soon reveal that each strand of their mutual bilateral relations has had a troubled past, the historical examination of which is essential to find clues for the possible future course of their relationship. It is a relationship that is bound to influence significantly the geopolitical contours of the 21st century. It is with the background of this conviction that this book has been mooted— to enable an informed comprehension of the forces at work in the evolving saga of the triangular relationship between the world's most powerful nation, the world's largest nation, and the world's largest democracy.

1 | The US-India Relationship

SECTION I

THE PAST

For too long during the past century, differences over domestic policies and international purposes kept India and the US estranged. But with the end of the Cold War, the rise of the global economy and the changing demographics in both of our countries, new opportunities have arisen for a partnership between our two great democracies.

US Secretary of State Condoleezza Rice
Washington DC, 13 March 2006

The estrangement so succinctly articulated by the US Secretary of State lasted for the better part of half a century, and came to an end only with the demise of the Cold War. Senator Daniel Patrick Moynihan of New York, a former US Ambassador to India, described it even more dramatically as "half a century of misunderstandings, miscues and mishaps".

In the six decades since India's Independence in 1947, Indo-US relations have gone through phases from cool (40s), to cold (50s), to lukewarm (60s), to ice-cold (70s), to indifferent (80s), to rediscovering and warming up to each other (90s) and thereafter, in the current decade, to the closest ever.

Normal logic dictated that given the common heritage of a colonial past from Britain, India and the US would have found a lot more in common in the August of 1947 when India emerged free from the shackles of British colonialism to sovereign, independent existence in the comity of nations. However, that was not to be. An America emerging from the ruins of a 'hot' war now found itself right in the midst of a Cold War in which it was desperately seeking "allies". A newly-independent India on the other hand, emerging onto the world stage a few years later after the same war, had different ideas. She did not wish to become a pawn in the ensuing rivalry between the two post-WWII superpowers—the US and the Soviet Union—preferring to chart her own independent course in foreign affairs.

It was not all a matter of altruism. There was a clear, cold and pragmatic angle to this decision. Even though headed towards the path of democracy as a governing ideology for the nascent nation, India's new leadership was acutely conscious of the physical distance that separated it from the USA, in stark contrast to the physical proximity—and cold reality—that two communist giants inhabited her immediate geographical neighbourhood, hovering menacingly in the North and East—one separated by a thin stretch of the Afghan 'panhandle' known as the Wakhan corridor and the other by an increasingly pregnable and penetrable Himalayan range of mountains. An alliance with the US, based solely on a shared political ideology, would have brought India into immediate, direct and totally unnecessary conflict with two of its largest and geographically immediate neighbours. Thus, it was more than just a case of being repelled from each other simply on account of a shared ideological magnetic polarity; it was more the desire of a newly-born country to avoid unnecessary confrontation with two of her largest, closest, and ideologically different neighbours. Moreover, India's new leaders, having secured India's Independence from Britain after two centuries of protracted struggle, were not about to barter away the hard-won freedom by another kind of servitude, based on post-war power politics.

To the US desperately in search for 'allies' in this war against the overarching evil of communism, India's dogged determination to remain equidistant from the emerging rival power blocs was perceived as nothing short of being downright "Immoral".[1] It was the then equivalent of today's 'Axis-of-Evil', except that communism at that time was seen by the US as the ultimate agglomeration of all evil. This pretty much set the tone for the next half century of the US-India relations, made worse by a rapidly growing friendship between the US and Pakistan, the breakaway nation whose very manner of birth had set a tone of bitter relations with India. During this period it was a simple zero-sum game. The closer Pakistan got to the US, the greater was the US estrangement with India. Determined to teach India a lesson for her espousal of what later came to be known as 'Non-alignment',

---

1.   The expression actually used by US Secretary of State John Foster Dulles in relation to India's decision to stay away from power bloc alignments.

the US rarely missed an opportunity to oppose, criticise or condemn India in international forums, or exact a heavy price for the pithiest assistance sought and offered. India reciprocated in kind—either individually, or collectively through NAM—by criticising the US on issues ranging from her involvement in Vietnam to support for the Anglo-French invasion of Suez to the policy of "constructive engagement" with the South African racist regime in South Africa which encouraged the perpetuation of apartheid. The list of Indo-US mutual recriminations was endless. As US Under Secretary for Political Affairs Nicholas Burns[2] put it "The US was, during the Cold War, the ultimate aligned nation, and India, the ultimate non-aligned nation."

Pandit Nehru visited the US in October 1949 and was invited to address a joint session of Congress. He acknowledged the debt that India owed to the US for having borrowed some of the fundamental principles of the American Constitution, especially those relating to basic human rights—justice, liberty, equality and the rule of law, in India's own draft Constitution (formally adopted in the following year). While openly appealing for assistance in the development of her industry and agriculture to improve the lot of her teeming millions, Pandit Nehru was very clear about not entering into any formal alliance to achieve this and said so in as many words: "We do not seek any material advantage in exchange for any part of our hard-won freedom", he said, in a clear reference on pursuing an independent course in foreign policy.

Through much of the 50s, the US helped India with export of food grains, in what came to be known infamously as "ship-to-mouth" supplies under the PL 480 programme.[3] More significantly, though, the US provided agricultural assistance, including hybrid seed technology, which eventually led to the Green Revolution and to India's self-sufficiency in food grain needs in subsequent decades. During this period, the US also appreciated the constructive role played by India in negotiating POW exchanges between

---

2. Speech at Asia Society, New York on 18 October 2005.

3. Later renamed "Food-for-Peace" programme which allowed the US to receive, and hold, payments for these supplies in local currency in India, thereby obviating the burden to pay for these supplies in hard currency. Besides using these funds for meeting administrative and logistic expenses of its Missions in India, the US also used them for funding scholarship programmes for US scholars in India.

the US and North Korea in the aftermath of the Korean War.[4] President Eisenhower's 5-day visit to India in December 1959, which was expected to allay some misgivings that the two nations had in bilateral relations, turned out to be largely symbolic. The US was not happy with India's growing commitment to non-alignment, as indeed India was unhappy with the growing military ties between the US and Pakistan. Interestingly, in foreign affairs, one of the major issues of contention between India and the United States was the US's continued recognition of the KMT regime in Taiwan as representing China, while India consistently argued in the UN, and with the US, that the government in Beijing (then called Peking) be given its rightful seat in the councils of the UN. In the ensuing years, India also became stridently critical of the US intervention in Vietnam, which irked the US so much that President Lyndon Johnson even thought of cutting off food aid to India in retaliation.

The unresolved question of Kashmir was another factor in the US-India relationship. Until the end of the Cold War, the US stance on Kashmir was highly partisan, in blind support of ally Pakistan, irrespective of the merits of the issue. Using its dominant position and influence in the UN, the US tried more than once to settle the issue in Pakistan's favour, only to be thwarted in every such attempt by a Soviet veto in India's favour. Actions such as these only helped exacerbate the US fears and generate misgivings in its foreign policy establishment about the genuineness of India's policy of non-alignment. For India, it was just a matter of national interest.

Faced with a highly unexpected attack by China across the Himalayan border in the winter of 1962, India urgently sought help from the US in its hour of dire national need. The timing was particularly unfortunate. It happened to coincide with the Cuban Missile crisis and the Kennedy Administration was too preoccupied in grappling with it to pay any serious attention to what was happening in the antipodes, and that too involving a non-aligned country which took great pride in distancing itself from superpowers, particularly the US. Still the US did provide some help—even if too little and too late—and restricted mostly to military software and intelligence sharing. It made no

---

4. India did so in her capacity as the Chairman of the Neutral Nations' Repatriation Commission (NNRC) set up to oversee POW exchanges.

impact on the final outcome of the conflict, but did earn the US a few rare brownie points in the perceptions of the Indian public.

For the limited assistance that the US had offered to India in the 1962 War with China, it expected a resolution of the Kashmir problem, albeit on terms favourable to its ally, Pakistan. Clearly, this was not a price India was willing to pay, especially when it had a watertight case with the entirely legal (in terms of international law) accession of the state to India. An increasingly impatient Pakistan, now firmly in the grip of its military generals and with its arsenals overflowing with the state-of-the-art military equipment supplied free by the US, felt that the time was now ripe to deliver a crushing blow to India—demoralised by a humiliating defeat in the 1962 war with China. Thus, Operation Gibraltar was conceived which led to the India-Pakistan War of 1965.[5] Initial victories in the Rann of Kutch by Pakistan forces reinforced the belief that India was now vulnerable, and the Kashmir fruit just ripe for plucking—and hence the opening of another front in Kashmir to wrest control of the Province from India. India counterattacked along the international border and soon Indian security forces were poised at the immediate outskirts of Lahore. An anxious US urgently sought Soviet intervention to save its ally and peace was brokered at Tashkent in Uzbekistan (then a Soviet province in Asiatic Russia). Repeated US assurances to India that the arms supplied to Pakistan were meant only to counter communist aggression were belied and Indian protests ignored. More interestingly, the US even chose to turn a blind eye to the rapidly developing close ties of friendship between Pakistan and China in the aftermath of the India-China war of 1962. While this new-found friendship was well-anchored in the timeless principle of one's enemy's enemy being a friend, what was less explicable was the tacit US acceptance of this relationship. After all Pakistan's *raison d'etre* for being a US ally was its commitment to the US's professed determination to halt the spread of communism spearheaded by the Soviets and the Chinese. Hence, the membership of Baghdad Pact, SEATO and CENTO[6]

---

5. Given free to Pakistan by the US by virtue of its membership of the Baghdad Pact, SEATO and (later) CENTO.

6. Baghdad Pact: Formed 1955, with Iraq, Iran, Turkey, Pakistan, the US, and the UK. In 1958, Iraq withdrew and the name was changed to CENTO. In 1979, Iran and Pakistan withdrew and CENTO was dissolved. SEATO was formed in 1954 with headquarters in Bangkok, Thailand. Membership: the US, the UK, France, Australia, NZ, Thailand, Pakistan, the Philippines. Pakistan withdrew (1973), France withdrew (1974). SEATO dissolved: 1977.

and the generous arms transfers by the US to Pakistan in terms of these pacts. And yet Pakistan was now warming up to a nation it was supposed to "contain" under these pacts. China gave generous moral and diplomatic support to Pakistan in the 1965 war with India and indicated more than once its willingness to provide arms and equipment to that country. Meanwhile, China ratcheted up pressure on India at several points along the Tibet border, especially in the Chumbi Valley near Sikkim (with aim of severing India's northeast by choking off the "Chicken's Neck") and along Arunachal Pradesh, threatening Tawang. When China finally threatened India with an open ultimatum that it would attack along the Sino-Indian border, the US acted to deter the Chinese with a clear warning that any such action could invite US intervention in East Asia.[7]

Soon after India's defeat in the 1962 border war with China, the latter tested its nuclear weapon in 1964. The deteriorating relationship with China and the increasing threat posed by the growing Sino-Pak *entente*, followed by the 1965 and 1971 wars with Pakistan is what appear to have led India's strategic planners to start thinking in terms of a nuclear deterrent. In 1965 itself there was strong Chinese support to Pakistan in the war with India, while the US did little to restrain its ally, but the situation in 1971 was radically different—with open moral, material and diplomatic support extended liberally to Pakistan both by China as well as the US.[8] Could India then be blamed for testing a 'Peaceful Nuclear Explosion' (PNE) in 1974?[9] Having been denied any kind of a 'nuclear umbrella' by the West in the aftermath of the 1964 Chinese n-test, India really had little option left in the matter. Yet her restraint was exemplary. The 1974 test was simply to let the world know that India possessed the wherewithal for developing a nuclear weapon even though it had no intention of doing so, and indeed did not, until the dictates of circumstance forced her to quarter of a century later. At any rate, the US did impose severe sanctions on India after the 1974 PNE, which did not help improve the bilateral relations that had already reached abysmal depths in 1971. US National Security Adviser, Henry Kissinger, visited India in October 1974

---

7. *Foreign Relations of the United States; 1964-1968*, Vol.3: 203 (US Government Printing Office 1989).

8. In India this was widely referred to at the time as the 'Washington-Islamabad-Peking Axis'.

9. The yield of the 1974 test was estimated at 12-15 kilotonnes (Hiroshima was 12 kt).

to tell Prime Minister Indira Gandhi—"Congrats, you did it, now what do we do from blowing up the world." Mrs. Gandhi left New Delhi the same day as Dr. Kissinger arrived, leaving him to meet his Indian counterpart at the appropriate level required in terms of strict protocol.

Even when Pakistan launched a genocidal attack against its own Eastern half in 1971, the US turned a blind eye to the atrocities despite repeated reports by her own diplomats, especially those stationed in Dacca (now Dhaka).[10] When the 1971 hostilities spilled across the highly porous border and millions of refugees fled to India in search of shelter and security, a hapless Indian Prime Minister travelled to Washington to appeal for help from President Nixon. The President gave her a cold reception; she was humiliated and the epithets later used to describe the meeting, available from recently declassified State Department documents, defy all canons of civilised dialogue, not to speak of Presidential decorum befiting a sitting occupant of the White House.[11] To make matters worse, in a crass display of modern-day gunboat diplomacy, the US despatched elements of the Seventh Fleet, led by nuclear-armed USS Enterprise, to the Bay of Bengal to threaten and intimidate India. As if that was not enough, the then Secretary of State, Henry Kissinger, did his utmost to provoke the Chinese leadership into attacking India[12] while, at the same time, personally calling the Indian Ambassador in Washington DC to tell him in no uncertain terms that if China attacked India (to help Pakistan), the US should not be expected to come to India's help. In the event, China did not heed Kissinger's gratuitous "advice" and the final outcome preceded any action that the US Seventh Fleet could possibly have taken, with some 93,000 soldiers of the Pakistan Army surrendering to the Joint Command of Indian defence forces and Bangladesh liberation forces. Despite every

---

10. The 'Blood' telegrams—classified dispatches sent by Dacca-based US Consul General Archer Blood to the State Dept., Washington DC.

11. According to the declassified conversation transcript (5 November 1971), shortly after a meeting with Prime Minister Indira Gandhi, Nixon said: "We really slobbered over the old witch". Chimed in Kissinger: "The Indians are bastards anyway". In an interview to NDTV, a private Indian TV news channel on 1 July 2005, Kissinger expressed regret over these statements: "I regret that these words were used. I have extremely high regard for Mrs Gandhi as a statesman," he said. (Source: BBC).

12. "I think we've got to tell [the Chinese] that some movement on their part...toward the Indian border could be very significant." On December 8, Nixon and Kissinger agreed to transfer planes to Pakistan and to tell the Chinese that "if you are ever going to move this is the time." (Source: National Security Archives, Washington DC).

US effort to force an opposite outcome, with or without help from China, her close ally lost its eastern half, which became the newest nation of Bangladesh. This, naturally, greatly angered the US. Nixon, Kissinger and Co. were livid.[13]

To ensure her security in the event of a highly-likely two-front war—Pakistan and China, with active US backing—India signed a Treaty of Peace and Friendship with the Soviet Union in August 1971, which upset the US greatly. India was accused of having summarily jettisoned non-alignment by joining the "enemy" camp. For India, it was clearly an insurance—perhaps the only available—against the frighteningly formidable and clearly-emerging 'Beijing-Islamabad-Washington Axis'.

A word about the background to the events of 1971. General elections in Pakistan in 1971 had returned Sheikh Mujibur Rahman's Awami League party to power on the basis of its overwhelming victory in the country's more populous eastern wing. The West Pakistan dominated military and civil institutions refused to accept the electoral verdict and launched an unprecedented repression of their own countrymen in the east. The country's eastern half rose in revolt, giving birth to a liberation movement, the 'Mukti Bahini'. The brutal crackdown in her eastern wing by Pakistan resulted in the millions of Bengali refugees fleeing across the border to India. To Nixon and Kissinger, this was simply an irritating sideshow, militating against their grander designs of using Pakistan as the conduit for opening up relations with China and drive a wedge between the two communist giants—the USSR and PRC.

The rest of the 70s saw Indo-US relations in much the same negative mould, except that they had fallen to such abysmal depths (in 1971) from where there was no way to go but up. Such an opportunity presented itself with the advent of new administrations in both countries following national elections. A new (non-Congress) government assumed power in New Delhi in March 1977 and a Democrat, Jimmy Carter, became the US President in January 1977. The new Indian Prime Minister, Morarji Desai, and his Foreign Minister, Atal Bihari Vajpayee, were both pro-West in their outlook, and both Washington and New Delhi thought the time was

---

13   In his present *avatar*, according to Kissinger: "The US recognises that India is a global
     power, that is a strategic partner of the US on the big issues".

now propitious to get the relations back to some semblance of normalcy befiting the largest and most powerful democracies of the world. President Carter paid a visit to India in January 1978 and the "Delhi Declaration" was signed with a ritualistic commitment to peace, democracy etc., but when it came to the nuts and bolts of, for example, supplying uranium for the Tarapur Atomic Plant,[14] the US held back more than it gave. An unintended, and uncomplimentary, gaffe by President Carter, unaware that microphones had been switched off at a large public gathering, did not help matters.

In any case, this attempt at getting Indo-US relations back to an even keel was short lived. A year later, in 1979, when the Soviet Union invaded Afghanistan, India was initially critical of the invasion but then abstained from a key vote in the UN where the Soviet action was condemned.[15] Pakistan, now having re-emerged as a 'frontline state' in the context of the new situation in Afghanistan, again became the recipient of generous doles of the US economic and military aid, including sophisticated F-16 aircraft, thereby once again upsetting the delicate arms balance on the subcontinent and setting off an arms race. India had to match these weapons for self-defence, given the proven track record of Pakistan having used US-supplied weaponry against India without inviting any serious objection from the supplier. With the US unwilling to sell weaponry to India, India turned to the Soviet Union and, to a lesser extent, to France and a few other selected countries for such military hardware as was necessary to offset Pakistan's sophisticated armoury generously refurbished by the US.

For a while in the 80s, it seemed that Indo-US relations had fallen back to their familiar old pattern, hostage inextricably again to the Pakistan factor. The only partial silver lining to these grey clouds came by way of a reasonably amicable meeting between (a re-elected) Prime Minister Indira Gandhi and President Reagan in 1982, followed by the US not objecting to France supplying uranium for the Tarapur Reactor. In 1984, the US even agreed to expand technology transfers to India (except for dual-use

---

14   A 320 MW reactor built with the US help in 1963 in Tarapur (Maharashtra State).

15.   In his book *The March of Folly in Afghanistan*, author Jagat Mehta describes it as "demonstrating our fidelity to the time tested friendship" with the Soviet Union. More aptly, it could perhaps be called as payback for Soviet support to India during the height of the crisis in the Indo-Pak War of 1971.

technology, as determined by the US), and in 1987 even permitted India to purchase a Cray Supercomputer, albeit a highly watered-down version.[16]

It took no less than the end of the Cold War another two decades later before the US could actually bring itself to take an unblinkered view of its relationship with India, genuinely de-hyphenated from its (now no longer the same) ties with Pakistan. The first evidence of this came during the 1999 Kargil War, initiated by Pakistan through *jihadis* infiltrated across the Line of Control (LOC) in Kashmir. Soon it became clear enough to the US intelligence outfits that most, if not all, of them were actually members of Pakistan's regular defence forces, not indigenous 'freedom fighters' as Pakistan stridently claimed. When (the then) Prime Minister of Pakistan, Nawaz Sharif, visited the US soon afterwards for help to defuse the situation, he was confronted by President Clinton with enough hard evidence, that the LOC had been violated by Pakistan and was told that its troops must withdraw back to its side of the LOC. This was perhaps the first ever indication that the US was now prepared to judge an issue between India and Pakistan on merits rather than blind and unquestioned support to an ally.

The end of the Cold War brought other factors into play between India and the US. Pakistan's role as an US ally underwent a fundamental transformation in US perceptions. With the Soviet Union gone and international communism in considerable disarray, SEATO and CENTO no longer relevant (eventually dissolved, out of redundancy, in 1977), the US was finally free to chart a new relationship with India, no longer subject to Pakistan's sensibilities or overriding concerns. India did not take long to reciprocate. In 1991, US warplanes refueled in Bombay during the Gulf War and soon thereafter the first ever Indo-US Naval Steering Committee was set up. The Kickleighter proposals of 1991 envisaged military to military cooperation and the pursuit of "a common policy of gradually strengthening ties towards expanded cooperation and partnership by the end of this decade". The objectives included joint training, military to military contacts and formation of Executive Steering Groups. Between 1992 and 1997, Indian and the US Navies conducted four joint exercises. In 1995, the "First Framework for US-India Defense Relationship" was

---

16. To ensure that a supercomputer intended for weather forecasting and cyclone warnings was not diverted for military purposes.

drawn up, and soon thereafter an Indo-US Defence Policy Group (DPG) was established. Regular joint exercises involving the army, navy, air force and marines take place now between India and the US.

Perhaps of even greater significance is that the end of the Cold War saw the beginnings of a changing definition of that four-letter word "ASIA" in the US perceptions—from the State Department to the Pentagon, and from media to academia and thence to the general public largely educated by them. Until then, Asia in the American geographic dictionary comprised Japan, Korea, China (actually Taiwan, until Nixon's great discovery in 1972), Vietnam and that old American colony, the Philippines. The Soviet invasion of Afghanistan in 1979 changed that somewhat. Now there were countries at the other end of Asia which had to be counted. The vast landmass in between, comprising some one-seventh of humanity, still had to await discovery by America. That came about only with the end of the Cold War.

As far as India was concerned, the end of the Cold War happened, fortuitously, to coincide with the start of India's era of radical and rapid economic reforms. The accompanying measures aimed at opening up the economy and removing a whole host of tariff and non-tariff barriers opened up a market of over 300 million middle class to US entrepreneurs and the liberalised norms for foreign direct investment (FDI) attracted both individual as well as institutional investors. More than the end of the Cold War per se, it was this coincidental liberalisation of India's economy that was largely responsible for a paradigm shift in Indo-US relations. The results were self-evident. Bilateral trade which stood at a mere $5.6 billion in 1990 grew to $14.4 billion within a decade (2000) and has more than doubled since then to $41.6 billion last year (2007). Similarly, foreign direct investment (FDI) from the US in India which was US $11.3 million in 1991 grew to US $4.1 billion in August 2004, recording an increase at a compound rate of 57.5 per cent per annum.

The credit for this qualitative transformation in Indo-US relations goes largely to President Bill Clinton who took some bold steps towards the end of his second term to reach out to India. He was the first US President to visit India (March 2000) since the relatively unfruitful visit by President Carter in 1978. The "Vision Statement" signed during his visit laid the unmistakable sinews of a strengthened friendship that was transformed a few years down the line into a strategic partnership by his Republican successor, thereby making it abundantly clear that it enjoyed bipartisan support.

The 1990s also witnessed the phenomenon of increased participation of the growing Indian-American community in contributing towards the qualitative enhancement of Indo-US relations. The over million strong community—most of whom came in the earlier decades as students and researchers—had worked their way up to become the most affluent recent immigrant community in per capita terms.[17] While they were not yet quite ready to participate directly in the American political process, they did use their powers of suasion with their legislators when it came to issues pertaining to the US relations with India. The first manifestation of this was by way of a Congressional Caucus on India, which was founded in 1993. Starting with humble beginnings, it has a membership of 176 (115 Democrats and 61 Republicans) at the time of this writing and is the largest country-related Caucus in the House of Representatives. Similarly, in the US Senate there is a 'Friends of India' group with a membership of 37 (19 Republicans and 18 Democrats).

The next major watershed in Indo-US bilateral relations came after the unfortunate bombing of the Twin World Trade Towers in New York on 11 September 2001 when both countries 'rediscovered' each other after falling victim to the forces of *jihadi* fundamentalism—something the US had consistently ignored until it knocked at its own front door in the forenoon of what has since become known only by its numerical acronym, "9-11". Little wonder that the late Senator Daniel Patrick Moynihan, speaking on the subject said: "As America reacts to the mass murder of 9/11 and prepares for more, it would do well to consider how much terror India endured in the second half of the last century." He was referring to the systematic diversion of Islamic militants—made redundant after the Soviet withdrawal from Afghanistan in February 1989—across the LOC

---

17.   According to the US Census Bureau, among all the listed ethnic groups, Indian Americans (called "Asian Indians") outperform all other racial/ethnic groups in most measures of socio-economic achievement. They have the highest educational rates—64 per cent have college degrees while 13 per cent have an advanced degree like law, medical, or doctorate degree. They have the highest median family income and the highest rate of working in a High-Skill Occupation like an executive, professional, technical, or upper management.

in Kashmir as part of Pakistan's policy of "bleeding India with a thousand cuts". Training camps set up in Pakistan-occupied Kashmir, just across from the Indian state of Jammu and Kashmir, served as the staging posts for infiltrating these militants in the name of *jihad*. To the outside world, Pakistan sought to portray this as an internal revolt by Kashmiris on the Indian side for freedom from Indian rule. Thousands of innocent lives have been lost—involving men, women and children, besides security forces—ever since this cross-border infiltration was launched in the early 90s and continues to this day, though greatly reduced. Meanwhile, the minority Hindu communities in Kashmir have been forced to leave their homes in the Valley and are living as refugees in camps elsewhere in their own country.

Not surprisingly, therefore, India was among the first nations to empathise with the US after the events of 9/11, having been the victim of the same forces of Islamic fundamentalism in the name of *jihad*. India offered unconditional support to the US in its war on terrorism including the use of military facilities.[18] This became evident during the launch of Operation Enduring Freedom in the aftermath of 9/11, which saw US military aircraft and warships being regularly refuelled in India. Later Indian warships escorted US naval vessels through the Straits of Malacca in support of Operation Enduring Freedom. India's response to 9/11 galvanised the bilateral military relationship into a "multidimensional relationship, deeply rooted in an appreciation of common strategic interests" which translates today into regular joint military exercises by the armies, navies and air forces of the two countries,[19] regular exchange of personnel for higher training and intensified interaction at the highest levels of the military commands. It is noteworthy that, India is among the few countries in the world that endorsed the National Missile Defence programme unveiled by the Bush Administration in May 2001. A Joint Working Group (JWG) on Terrorism has been set up which meets regularly twice a year—in New Delhi and Washington respectively—to exchange intelligence and discuss counter-terrorism measures.

---

18.   US sanctions against India were removed in September 2001.

19.   These are the 'Malabar' series of exercises by the navies, the 'Yudh Abhyas' by the armies, and the 'Cope' series by air forces of the two countries.

SECTION II

CHALLENGES AND OPPORTUNITIES

The US has undertaken a transformation in its bilateral relationship with India...
We are the two largest democracies, committed to political freedom protected
by representative government. We have a common interest in the free flow of
commerce, including through the vital sea lanes of the Indian Ocean. Finally, we
share an interest in fighting terrorism and in creating a strategically stable Asia.

President George Bush
March 2002

US Secretary of State Condoleezza Rice was quoted at the beginning of the chapter as saying that "with the end of the Cold War, the rise of the global economy and the changing demographics in both of our countries, new opportunities have arisen for a partnership between our two great democracies". Add to this President Bush's assertion quoted above and it becomes clear that both the challenges as well as the opportunities in the emerging bilateral relationship between India and the US are centred around economics, demography, democracy, the fight against terrorism, and strategic cooperation in Asia. We will discuss each of these in the rest of this section.

As has been stated earlier, the end of the Cold War in the late 80s and early 90s happened to coincide with the advent of economic liberalisation in India. In part it was accidental, because the economy had started showing signs of extreme strain after years of bureaucratic controls internally and high tariffs externally, and in part it was also a direct outcome of the collapse of the Soviet bloc of countries who had long been India's main source of technology and barter trade. Now regulated by the capitalist forces of supply-and-demand rather than ideological considerations, this 'comfort zone' of preferential trade at artificially-fixed prices was no longer an option available for India. The Eastern bloc countries no longer needed second-quality Indian consumer goods, just as India no longer needed second-rate Eastern bloc technologies. It worked miracles for India. The moment shackles began being removed from the Indian economy, tariffs lowered and foreign direct investment encouraged, the economy started showing 5-7 per cent growth in GNP in the first decade (nearly double the so-called "Hindu" rate of growth of 3-4 per cent in the previous decades) to be topped by 7 to 9 per cent in the years of the new millennium. Foreign exchange reserves which had fallen to the abysmal low of under $2 billion in 1991, enough barely to cover one month's imports, grew to $40 billion by the end of 2000 and stand at well over $300 billion today[20] and are rising. Indeed, how desperate the situation had reached is clear from the fact that in March 1991 India was forced to sell 20 tonnes of gold in the London market simply to tide over its immediate and most pressing needs.

With a middle class of some 300 million—or the same size as the entire population of the US—India obviously offers vast market opportunities—both for export trade as well as foreign direct investment (FDI). US multinationals, banks and financial institutions, as well as other entrepreneurs have been quick to see and seize the opportunity to move in quickly in the years after economic liberalisation took effect. The results are self-evident.[21]

- From a modest US$ 5.6 billion in 1990, the bilateral trade between India and the US has increased to US$ 41.6 billion in 2007 or more than six-fold growth in a span of 17 years.

- India's exports to the US grew from US$ 21.8 billion in 2006 to US$ 24 billion in 2007, an increase of over 10 per cent.

- US exports to India grew from US$ 10 billion in 2006 to US$ 17.6 billion in 2007, an increase of by 76 per cent.

- Indo-US bilateral trade is projected to grow by another 50 per cent over the 2007 figures to about $60 billion during 2008.

According to Goldman Sachs, at current rates of economic growth, India will become the world's 5th largest economy by 2025 (after the US, China, Japan, and Germany), but by 2050, with China having overtaken the US, it will be the 3rd largest, after those two countries. Some current indicators already support part of this prognosis. The US is today India's largest trading partner and the biggest overseas investor, but China is poised to overtake the US and become India's largest trading partner within the next year or two. The same will not hold true for Chinese investment in India, but the same period will see a considerable increase in Indian investment in the US.

---

20. Fourth largest in the world after China, Japan and Russia.
21. US Census Bureau, Foreign Trade Division, Data Dissemination Branch, Washington D.C. 20233.

Table 1.1

Top Five Economies

2005	2025	2050
US	US	China
Japan	China	US
Germany	Japan	India
France	Germany	Japan
UK	India	Brazil

Source: Goldman Sachs BRICs report, December 2005.

Unlike the enormously skewed trade imbalance between the US and China, compounded by the tension surrounding the undervaluation of the Chinese currency, the US has no fundamental differences in its growing trade relationship with India. The margin of trade differential is not something that troubles the US, and the Indian currency's value is determined entirely by market forces. In international economic forums such as the ongoing Doha round, the US and India are increasingly seen to work together to harmonise their respective positions. In other words, the US feels quite comfortable in its economic relations with India, in contrast to China where it feels intimidated if not threatened.

The US is the largest investing country in India in terms of FDI approvals, actual inflows, and portfolio investment. The US investments cover almost every sector in India, which is open for private participants. The stock of actual FDI inflow increased from US $11.3 million in 1991 to US $4132.8 million as on August 2004 recording an increase at a compound rate of 57.5 per cent per annum. The FDI inflows from the US constitute about 11 per cent of the total actual FDI inflows into India. The main areas are:[22]

- Fuels (power and oil refining): 36 per cent
- Telecoms (paging, cellular and basic phone services): 10.6 per cent
- Electronics and Computer Software: 9.5 per cent
- Food processing : 9.4 per cent, and
- Services sector (fin. and non-finance): 8.3 per cent

With a highly comfortable level of foreign exchange holdings ($316 billion as of mid-2008), India is encouraging its entrepreneurs to open up a regime of

22.   *http://www.economywatch.com/foreign-direct-investment/india-united-states.html*

Indian investments overseas which would also help to provide Indian industry much-needed access to new markets and technologics and contribute to their export competitiveness globally. The US is the most preferred destination accounting for a fifth of the total. Up to September 2004, the total approved Indian investment abroad was over US$ 11 billion, of which the US share was $2.2 billion. India's outgoing investments have largely been in the services sector (notably software development) and in manufacturing.[23]

A word about the nuclear factor in US-India relations. It is true that India's first tests in 1974, the PNE, drew prompt US condemnation, followed by sanctions, and when after a quarter of century of nuclear restraint, the 'option' was eventually 'weaponised' in 1998, it drew even greater condemnation and more sanctions. But 1998 was not 1974, and the security environment in the world had greatly changed. What came out of it, and undoubtedly for the first time, was a genuine US desire to understand India's overriding security concerns that led to the 1998 tests. Outrageous as it may sound, when India "gate-crashed"[24] into the exclusive N-club, US-India relations assumed a much more pragmatic, down-to-earth shape. Once the initial claptrap of rollback-cap-eliminate died down, US Deputy Secretary of State, Strobe Talbott and India's Minister of External Affairs, Jaswant Singh sat down together to do some serious talking about the subject. Their in-depth and wide-ranging content can be judged from the fact that these discussions, held in a kind of roving Camp David retreat style in 14 rounds took place in seven different countries over a period of two years between 1999 and 2001.[25] The end result of it was a more realistic appreciation of India's wider security concerns,[26] which in part, and not entirely coincidentally, overlapped those of the US

---

23. Total foreign direct investment (FDI) into India surged to over US$ 25 billion in 2007-08 and the country's foreign exchange reserves crossed US$ 316 billion as of mid-June 2008. (*Source:* CII, New Delhi).

24. This expression was frequently used by western media to refer to India's 1998 N-tests, as if China in 1964, or Britain and France in the 50s, had received formal invitations to join the nuclear club.

25. Strobe Talbott (2004). *Engaging India—Diplomacy, Democracy & the Bomb*. Brookings Institution.

26. India's 1998 N-tests were a security blanket against: (a) a nuclear China on its east (with whom it had fought a bitter war and lost thousands of square miles of territory, with a lot more claimed), and (b) a nuclear Pakistan on its west, outfitted by China and North Korea, actively peddling its N-wares to the very countries listed in US's 'Axis-of-Evil', besides others such as Libya, Syria, etc.

itself in the aftermath of 9/11. This explains the systematic removal of US sanctions against India and the subsequent enthusiasm shown by the US in cooperating with India in the field of civilian nuclear energy. By agreeing to India separating her civilian and military facilities with the latter being outside international safeguards, the US practically signaled its tacit *de facto* acceptance of India's NWS status. Now there is no talk of India signing the NPT, CTBT etc., any more, but only of making India a part of the solution. The point to be noted here is that India never was part of the problem—given her impeccable track record on nuclear proliferation, which is on record of surpassing that of any of the formal nuclear weapons States.

The path-breaking visit by President Bill Clinton in March 2000 did much to open a new chapter in bilateral relations, coming soon after the impartial stand taken by the US during the 1999 Kargil conflict between India and Pakistan. The 'Vision Statement' issued during the visit spoke of the "profound responsibility" of the two nations "to work together", adding that "our partnership of shared ideals leads us to seek a natural partnership of shared endeavors". More significantly, however, it acknowledged India's economic rise and political influence and pledged the US's desire to work together with India in the new century: "India and the United States will be partners in peace, with a common interest in and complementary responsibility for ensuring regional and international security. We will engage in regular consultations on, and work together for, strategic stability in Asia and beyond. We will bolster joint efforts to counter terrorism and meet other challenges to regional peace." In concrete terms, the "Agreed Principles" attached to the 'Vision Statement' provided for a multi-pronged approach to be put into action straightaway. These were:[27]

1. Institutionalising the dialogue between the United States and India at the highest level on a regular basis through bilateral 'Summits' in alternating capitals or elsewhere, including on the occasions of multilateral meetings, to review bilateral relations and consult on international developments and issues. It also provided for regular

---

27.   Website of the Embassy of India, Washington DC.

interaction at the Foreign Minister's level, officials' level and through mechanisms like the Joint Working Group (JWG) on Terrorism.[28]

2. Setting up of a US-India Financial and Economic Forum headed by the US Secretary of the Treasury and the Indian Finance Minister to deal with finance and investment issues, macroeconomic policy and international economic developments at regular intervals. Their meetings at the ministerial level would be supplemented by sub-Cabinet meetings and involve, as appropriate, the participation of the Securities and Exchange Commission (SEC), the Federal Reserve, the Council of Economic Advisors, and other officials of the US Government and the Securities and Exchange Board of India (SEBI), Reserve Bank of India, and other officials of the Government of India.

3. Starting a formal US-India Commercial Dialogue between the US Secretary of Commerce and India's Commerce Minister to develop linkages between Indian and American business communities. The dialogue encompasses regular government-to-government meetings which are held in conjunction with private sector meetings with the aim of: (a) facilitating trade, and (b) maximising investment opportunities across a broad range of economic sectors, including information technology, infrastructure, biotechnology, and services. Participation includes, as appropriate, representatives of other Cabinet agencies and ministries on both sides. Close contact is maintained with relevant business associations and chambers of commerce to pursue specific projects or sectoral issues of mutual interest.

4. Setting up of a US-India Working Group on Trade: The United States Trade Representative and India's Ministry of Commerce and other concerned Ministries/Departments of the Government of India engage in regular discussion to enhance cooperation on trade policy. As appropriate, individual trade issues are examined in greater depth with the participation of other agencies with corresponding responsibilities and through creation of sub-groups. The Group serves as a locus of consultation on a broad range of trade-related

---

28. The Joint Working Group on counter-terrorism had its highly-productive first meeting in February 2000 and agreed that the JWG should continue to meet regularly and become an effective mechanism for the two countries to share information and intensify their cooperation in combating terrorism. Eleven meetings have been held thus far.

issues, including those pertaining to the World Trade Organisation. The Group is open to inputs from the private sector (including trade policy issues identified in the US-India Commercial Dialogue) as appropriate.

5. The establishment of a Joint Consultative Group on Clean Energy and Environment which holds periodic ministerial/high level meetings to discuss collaborative projects, developing and deploying clean energy technologies, public and private sector investment and cooperation, and climate change and other environmental issues. The co-conveners of the Group are the Department of State of the United States and the Ministry of External Affairs of India.

As is evident, both in terms of its scope and breadth, these elements in the Vision Statement brought about a quantum jump in the qualitative relationship between the two countries, setting it on an unprecedented trajectory for the 21st century. After Bill Clinton, President George Bush who succeeded him, committed the US to a strategic partnership between India and the US. The meeting with the Indian Prime Minister Atal Bihari Vajpayee in November 2001 laid the cornerstone of future relations between the two countries, rooted in the determination to expand the breadth and intensity of the bilateral interaction. .

The results were dramatic and far-reaching. In January 2004, the US and India agreed to expand cooperation in the areas of civilian nuclear activities, civilian space programmes, high-technology trade, and missile defence. These areas of cooperation were designed to progress through a series of reciprocal steps that built on each other, and were termed as the 'Next Steps in the Strategic Partnership' or the NSSP. Clearly the US was beginning to get impressed with India's rapidly reforming and growth-oriented economy, a strong technical and industrial resource base, capable scientific and engineering manpower and its huge middle-income market—all functioning within the norms of a well-established and resilient democracy.

The 'democracy' dividend plays out in other arenas too. The US and India established a Virtual Coordination and Information Centre on September 22, 2005 to share best practices on democracy, identify opportunities for joint support, and highlight capacity-building training programmes.[29] This is an

---

29. Virtual Democracy Centre website *http://democracy.state.gov*

outcome of the Global Democracy Initiative agreed to during the summit of President Bush and PM Manmohan Singh on July 18, 2005. As part of this initiative the US and India are working to strengthen democratic capacity in societies who wish to become more open and pluralistic. The US and India are also cooperating closely under the auspices of the Community of Democracies, supporting UN electoral assistance programmes, and have each provided $10 million to the UN Democracy Fund.

In October 2005, India and the US signed a Science and Technology agreement as part of the series of pacts aimed at bringing the two countries together in areas such as health, space and information technology, basic sciences, energy, health and frontier areas such as nanotechnology, etc.

In an act more noteworthy for its underlying symbolism than perhaps its quantitative worth, an Indian Air Force aircraft delivered 25 tonnes of relief supplies for Hurricane Katrina victims at the Little Rock Air Force Base, Arkansas on September 13, 2005. The relief supplies comprised 3000 blankets, bed sheets, tarpaulins and personal hygiene items, besides a cash contribution of $5 million to the American Red Cross to help the victims of Hurricane Katrina disaster.

The biggest-ever joint naval exercises between India and the US were held in October 2003. The 10-day war games in the Arabian Sea steered clear of thorny issues such as simulated nuclear combat, officials said. Code named "Malabar" it began when the 1,092-foot (333-metre) aircraft carrier USS Nimitz led two American Aegis-class destroyers into Indian waters on September 25. The nuclear-powered Nimitz is the first US carrier to take part in joint exercises with nations outside the NATO. The joint exercise, 8th in a series between the two Navies and involved F-18 Hornets from the US side and British-designed Sea Harriers, which flew several sorties from the deck of India's aircraft carrier INS Viraat. More recently, in October 2007, Japan, Australia and Singapore joined India and the US in naval exercises in the Bay of Bengal. The exercises involve three aircraft carriers, two from the US—USS Nimitz and USS Kitty Hawk—and one from India, hundreds of military aircraft, destroyers, frigates and submarines. The exercises, which involved anti-piracy, anti-marine terrorism, air defence, surveillance and interception elements, drew a sharp reaction from China who saw it as an attempted 'encirclement' of China by a new 'axis-of-democracy'.

Prime Minister Manmohan Singh's July 2005 visit to Washington was significant for arriving at an agreement for civilian nuclear cooperation and paved the way for President Bush's 4-day visit to India in March 2006. Today, the US vows to "help India become a major world power in the 21st century". US-India relations are now conducted under the rubric of three major "dialogue" areas: strategic (including global issues and defence), economic (including trade, finance, commerce, and environment), and energy.

On the negative side, however, the US is still lukewarm to India's admission to United Nations Security Council (UNSC), while arguing strongly for the case of Japan and Germany. The challenge here lies in India being able to convince the US that her coming on board will be in the larger interests of the US and the free world, and in promoting democracy and human rights globally. Unlike the Cold War past, the independent mindset of India's leadership is no longer conditioned to an anti-US thermostat, but on the contrary looks to the US as a partner in containing the dangers of terrorism, fundamentalism and extremism, in preventing nuclear weapons falling into the hands of rogue regimes or terrorist groups, and in encouraging more free trade and investment. In all these areas and many more, India is a partner not a rival or obstacle. India, for example, is as interested as the US, if not more, in preventing nuclear proliferation and the opening up of nuclear Walmarts by state-supported individuals or entities. Contrary to popularly held perceptions, India is working very closely with the US in bringing the Doha Round to a successful conclusion. All these are pointers of a similarity of approach to critical international issues in which the US will always find a partner in India. What, however, the US will not find (if that is what it is looking for) is blind support for every US cause like unilateral regime change or physical intervention in member-states without legitimate UN authority. The case of Japan and Germany that the US so robustly espouses is precisely because it can be much more confident of their unquestioned support in the UN than India's. The downside of it, of course, is that China is hardly likely to ever agree to Japan's membership and as for Germany, is western Europe not already heavily overrepresented in the P-5? Above all, one has only to ask whether it is fair to deprive one-seventh of humankind of a legitimate voice in the highest council of the UN.

Another issue that is currently bedeviling India-US relations is the question of Iran. Many in the US feel that India should align its policies to conform to the current US policy towards Iran because of its nuclear ambitions. Since Iran is a signatory to the NPT, India went along with the western position, spearheaded by the US, in the IAEA. That is where India stops, refusing beyond that to jump on an all-inclusive anti-Iran US-driven bandwagon, for the simple reason that it militates against India's current national interest, besides past historic and civilisational links that India has with Iran. Thus, when an energy-starved India strikes a good deal for Iranian natural gas, even if it is to be piped overland through Pakistan no less, it does not wish to be pilloried by the US as a price for civilian nuclear cooperation, or anything else for that matter. The US forgets in such cases that India is a democracy too and there is an official opposition that sits in Parliament, ready at a moment's notice to put the Government on the mat for succumbing to the dictates of a foreign power at the cost of national interest. A case in point is that of the Indo-US agreement on civilian nuclear cooperation, even though it is overwhelmingly clear that it was in India's interest, the government has to battle recalcitrant Left parties who, simply out of what many have called a "visceral" dislike of the US, did not wish India to conclude the agreement.[30] India needs to be mindful of its relations with Iran for a variety of reasons that have nothing to do with the US. India's large Shia minority (and hence a vote bank for any political party) is one of them. Strategic depth is another—after all Pakistan parked its vulnerable air force during the 1971 Indo-Pak war, in Iran. Then, again, Iran borders Afghanistan as well as Pakistan, so India's geopolitical interest in that country is self-evident. In the end if, despite signing the NPT and in defiance of unrelenting US pressure, Iran still somehow manages to get 'the bomb' (whose pursuit it vigorously denies), the US only has itself to blame. After all it kept turning a blind eye all

---

30. At the time of this writing, the ruling UPA Government has decided to defy India's communist parties and press ahead with the 40-year agreement, extendable by 10 years, which commits the US to uninterrupted fuel supplies for Indian reactors even if it terminates its cooperation and to help create strategic fuel reserve for Indian safeguarded nuclear reactors. The leftists and the opposition's biggest objection that it ties down India not to do any further tests is unfounded. The Agreement provides for a consultative mechanism if termination of the pact is warranted due to any reason, including "changed security environment". This is the fallback arrangement if India is compelled to conduct a nuclear test in case its security is threatened, say from Pakistan and/or China.

these years to Pakistan's developing its "Islamic" bomb (with generous help from another NPT member nation) and to the flourishing export business that its architect, A.Q. Khan,[31] was running. Iran was one such beneficiary, besides Libya, Syria and Iraq.

SECTION III

THE WAY AHEAD

India is a great democracy and our shared values are the foundation of our good relations... We have made great strides in transforming America's relationship with India, a major power that shares our commitment to freedom, democracy, and the rule of law. In July 2005, we signed a bold agreement—a roadmap to realise the meaningful cooperation that had eluded our two nations for decades. India now is poised to shoulder global obligations in cooperation with the US in a way befitting a major power.

President George Bush
March 2006

The US President also said that "after years of estrangement, India and the US together surrendered to reality. They recognised an unavoidable fact—they are destined to have a qualitatively different and better relationship than in the past."

India and the US may have had a challenging past, but the future certainly is full of promise and hope. This optimistic prognosis flows from what has been stated in the earlier two sections and will now be summed up.

Once the Cold War was over, the Non-aligned Movement (NAM)—the long-time *bete noire* of the US—became largely redundant, even if belabouredly re-engineered by its erstwhile members to now represent the economic interests of the developing South *vis-à-vis* the developed North.[32] The contentious issues that brought the US into direct clash with India and other members of the NAM, especially their 'tilt' towards the former Soviet Union, had now disappeared. No matter what the post-Cold War reincarnation of a born-again NAM represents, it is no longer directed against the western world led by the US. As for economic issues—such as poverty alleviation, energy security and environmental concerns etc., it is now equally in US's interests to ensure that, as the sole surviving

---

31.   in a startling revelation on 4 July 2008, A.Q. Khan said that Pakistan supplied centrifuges to North Korea in 2000 with the complete knowledge of the Army, then headed by Pervez Musharraf as the country's Chief Executive as well as Army Chief.

32.   Especially in such forums as the WTO.

superpower, it is perceived in a positive light as contributing to the solution of such pressing issues affecting the future of the developing world. In other words, the US could possibly work with the broad aims and ideals of a reborn NAM that was simply not possible during the heady days of the Cold War. That NAM itself was misused by the likes of Fidel Castro as a platform to denounce the US was, of course, another matter, and may still happen with the likes of Hugo Chavez and Robert Mugabe around. But the bottom line now is that even though it was the original founder and main protagonist of NAM during the Cold War, India no longer accords the same political weightage to the movement and, at any rate, will never in the changed context allow it to be used as a vehicle to oppose the US or the West in general. So, the ghost of NAM as an irritant in developing Indo-US ties has all but disappeared.

A much bigger ghost lies buried too—that of Pakistan—as a factor militating against the development of friendly relations between India and the US. Once the Cold War was over, India was no longer 'tilted' towards the Soviet Union, and there was no more need for the US to 'tilt' towards Pakistan on any India-Pakistan issue. The US could finally 'de-hyphenate' its old India-Pakistan equation by virtue of which hitherto every issue concerning the relationship towards India had to weighed in terms of how it would affect Pakistan, or how Pakistan would react to it. This also explains the objective stance the US could afford to take during the 1999 Indo-Pak crisis over Kargil, and Pakistan clearly told to withdraw to its side of the LOC when the conflict between the two nuclear-armed neighbours threatened to get out of hand.

Pakistan's utility to the US as a 'frontline' state—against the spread of international communism during the Cold War and against the 'evil Soviet Empire' in the aftermath of the Afghanistan invasion in 1979—had evaporated by the early 90s. This state of affairs continued until the advent of 9/11, when Pakistan, once again out of the blue, became a 'frontline' state—albeit this time against another enemy whom both had befriended after 1979, namely the Taliban. The only difference was that after the Soviet departure from Afghanistan in 1989 and the end of the Cold War, the Taliban were abandoned by the US, but not by Pakistan, who carefully cultivated the group—in power or out—with the long-term aim to acquire 'strategic depth' in Afghanistan, indeed even going so far as to help them get into the driving seat of power in Kabul. The US had lost all interest in them until 9/11 when the nexus between them and the Al-Qaeda was clearly established and it was discovered that their operational base areas—from where all activity against the West (including the masterminding of 9/11 itself) was directed—lay in the border areas adjoining Pakistan and Afghanistan.[33] Worse still, ample evidence surfaced of the clandestine but active links between Pakistan's intelligence agency, the ISI, and the Taliban/Al-Qaeda combine. So while US Deputy Secretary of State Richard Armitage may or may not have actually promised to bomb Pakistan back to the stone age[34] unless it came on board in the US-led 'War on Terror' in the aftermath of 9/11, Musharraf clearly got the message of what was good for him and for the country that he ruled unelected. However, the Americans were not in for a free lunch. Musharraf also saw in this an opportunity—after all he needed money and arms, and more of both as time went on, to fight his former friends, the Taliban whom he was not only deserting but turning against to fight. Seven years and at least a reported $56 billion later not much has been achieved as far as the US is concerned,[35] the allied ISAF is still receiving a drubbing at the hands of the Taliban and Osama Bin Laden is still happily living in the area technically under Pakistani control with the likes of Mullah Omar and Ayman Al-Zawahiri to keep him company.

On the other hand, and in direct contrast, India has been playing an increasingly active role, ever since the advent of the Karzai Government (in the wake of 9/11) in the economic reconstruction of Afghanistan, thereby indirectly but indubitably supplementing the efforts of the US-led International Security Assistance Force (ISAF), albeit at the civilian level. Some of the key areas have been road construction, public health, education, telecommunications, and human resource development. Since August 2002 when India announced its first tranche of financial assistance of US$ 100 million for Afghanistan, India has already spent

---

33.   The Waziristan and FATA (Federally Administered Tribal Area) in Pakistan.

34.   Armitage was at pains to deny Musharraf's assertion, made on public TV, that he was left with no choice except to join the US led 'War on Terror' after 9/11, given that the alternative was for Pakistan to be "bombed back to the Stone Age".

35.   "From the American perspective, we've spent billions of dollars and have gotten far too little to show for it," said Joe Biden, Chairman of the US Senate Foreign Relations Committee on 25 June 2008 during hearings on a 'US strategy for Pakistan'.

over $750 million besides contributing to the World Bank-managed Afghan Reconstruction Trust Fund. Since then India has also gifted three civilian airliners to the Ariana Afghan Airlines besides cash subsidies to support the Afghan budget, deputation of doctors to Kabul and Mazar-e-Sharif for providing medical assistance, including the setting up of a camp for artificial limbs for Afghan soldiers. Fifty buses were provided by India to kick-start Kabul's road transport system. India has also been paying special attention to the human resource needs of the new government. Afghan police, civil servants, diplomats, doctors and paramedics numbering several hundreds are being trained in specialised Indian institutions. A computer training centre has been set up in Kabul for providing computer training to Afghan officials, besides the establishment of a LAN Network with internet access via VSAT in the office of the Foreign Minister of Afghanistan. India is also involved in the erection of a new seat of the national Parliament in Kabul.[36] In other words, whatever the US is trying to achieve militarily with ISAF in Afghanistan, India is helping achieve it with the process on economic reconstruction and building of civil society institutions. This is clearly because of an unstated but insuperable common interest in the war on terrorism and fundamentalism which both India and the United States are fighting on the same side. Despite the horrendous attack on the Indian Embassy in Kabul in July 2008 by a suicide bomber, in which India lost two senior diplomats, Prime Minister Manmohan Singh reiterated India's resolve and continued commitment to the people of Afghanistan and to the ongoing war on terror in that country.

The dawn of the 21st century has witnessed a reinvigorated bilateral Economic Dialogue, a greater thrust to the activities of the joint Defense Policy Group, expanded military exercises, launching of the India-US Global Issues Forum, starting a High Technology Cooperation Group (HTCG), and setting in motion a number of other initiatives designed to foster bilateral cooperation. Giving a renewed thrust to earlier initiatives and the launch of new ones, President Bush and then Prime Minister

---

36. According to the New York Times (July 10, 2008), India's "engagement has come at a mounting cost to the 4,000 Indian citizens working in Afghanistan. In the last two and a half years, an Indian driver for the road reconstruction team was found decapitated, an engineer was abducted and killed, and 7 members of the paramilitary force guarding Indian reconstruction crews were killed. Last year alone, the Indian Border Roads Organization came under 30 rocket attacks as it built the 124-mile stretch of road across Nimroz Province."

Vajpayee announced the Next Steps in Strategic Partnership (NSSP) in January 2004: a major initiative to expand high technology trade, dialogue on missile defence, and cooperation in space and civilian nuclear cooperation besides others.

Prime Minister Manmohan Singh's visit to Washington in July 2005 provided a fresh boost to the bilateral relationship and the drawing up of a new framework for even closer cooperation in the years ahead. Both agreed that an enhanced US-India relationship can make an important contribution to global stability, democracy, prosperity, and peace. The July visit also coincided with the completion of the NSSP initiative launched 18 months earlier, but both the US President and the Indian Prime Minister reiterated that the NSSP provides a basis for expanding bilateral activities and commerce in space, civil nuclear energy, and dual-use technology. Indeed, the US-India Civil Nuclear Cooperation initiative announced during the visit would not have been possible without the foundation laid by the completion of the NSSP.

Let us take a broad overview of the state of relations between the US and India in different areas:

Economy: A key area which has witnessed remarkable strides ever since the liberalisation of the Indian economy in the post Cold War period. Figures of quantum increases in bilateral trade and investment, which speak volumes for themselves, have already been provided earlier. A further boost to trade and investment in the coming days will be seen with the recent inauguration of a CEO Forum, comprising 20 chief executive officers from the most dynamic among US and Indian firms involved in enhancing the bilateral economic relationship. They represent a wide cross-section of industrial sectors, particularly those that have a stake in improving the commercial climate between India and the US. According to a senior US official: "This forum will serve as a channel to provide senior-level private sector input into discussions at the Economic Dialogue. Their input will help both countries make progress on key issues that will enhance economic growth and job creation and promote bilateral trade and investment. We see the creation of the CEO Forum as part of a more general commitment to enhancing the US-India Economic Dialogue. As the Indian economy grows and becomes increasingly interconnected with the world economy, our bilateral economic relationship has expanded beyond trade into new and increasingly complex areas that are having a profound impact on the economic outlook in the 21st century."[37]

The US-India Economic Dialogue referred to above has four tracks, namely, the Trade Policy Forum, the Financial and Economic Forum, the Environment Dialogue and the Commercial Dialogue. Each of these tracks is led by the respective US agency and Indian ministry. In addition, the Economic Dialogue has two sub-forums on biotechnology and information technology. The underlying idea is to widen economic opportunities and tackle any impediments given that both countries recognise the urgent need to modernise India's infrastructure as a prerequisite for the economy to sustain its current high rates of growth. Once impediments are speedily removed, the investment climate will continue to enjoy the requisite buoyancy that will be essential to attract the private capital necessary to fund infrastructure investment. It is recognised that this cuts both ways, to wit the high levels of economic growth are vital for India to meet its developmental goals and, in turn that stimulates the US private sector by providing its entrepreneurs more commercial opportunities.

Energy and the Environment: A US-India Energy Dialogue was also mooted during Prime Minister Manmohan Singh's US visit in July 2005 to promote trade and investment in the energy sector. Here the intention is to achieve faster results with the help of individual working groups devoted to oil and natural gas, electric power, coal and clean coal technology, energy efficiency, new and renewable energy technologies, besides civil nuclear energy. This will help India meet some of her more pressing needs in the energy sector while also safeguarding the environment through the promotion of cleaner, more efficient, affordable, and diversified energy technologies.

Democracy: The world's oldest and largest democracies have decided to join hands in helping countries on the threshold of democracy to make what sometimes appears to be a difficult and painful transition, given their earlier history of authoritarian rule. India and the US are actively engaged in a Global Democracy Initiative which draws on the US and Indian democratic traditions, institutions and practical experience to help build democratic institutions and strengthen foundations of civil society. In

---

37. US Under Secretary of State Nick Burns testifying before the US House of Representatives International Relations Committee on 8 September 2005.

terms of this initiative, both countries have pledged generous contributions to the new UN Democracy Fund which has as its mandate the building and nurturing of democratic institutions around the world.

Health: KPOs (Knowledge Process Outsourcing) from the US to India in the field of medicine, especially radiology, MRIs etc., has been flourishing for quite some time with enormous mutual benefits on both sides. Those are, of course, all private sector initiatives. At the official level, India and the US have drawn up the blueprint for active partnership in an effort to encourage the private sector to undertake greater efforts in the prevention, care, and treatment of people living with HIV/AIDS not only in India but other vulnerable countries like Sub-Saharan Africa. Lately protocols for the transfer of biomaterials and for clinical trials of medicines in India have also been worked out.

Disaster Response: In a classic case of cooperation between the militaries of the two countries for responding to an international disaster, the US and Indian navies worked in close concert during the tsunami disaster that struck many countries in South and Southeast Asia in December 2004. Together with Japan and Australia, the US and India formed a Core Group that cooperated closely to coordinate the initial international response. In the backdrop of the valuable experience gained during this exercise, the two countries have launched a US-India Disaster Response Initiative which will provide a basis for future India-US cooperation on disaster assistance, not just in the Indian Ocean region, but beyond.

Science and Technology: A Science and Technology Framework Agreement is in place which will supplement the activities of the US-India High-Technology Cooperation Group (HTCG) to provide for joint research and training, and the establishment of public-private partnerships. The US is also encouraging Indian participation in the fusion energy International Thermonuclear Experimental Reactor (ITER) project and the Generation IV International Forum, the work of which relates to advanced nuclear energy systems.

Space Cooperation: There has lately been increased bilateral cooperation in space exploration, satellite navigation and launch capabilities following the establishment of a US-India Working Group on Civil Space Cooperation.

Agricultural Alliance: With the current food crisis facing the world, the setting up of a US-India Knowledge Initiative on Agriculture, is very timely in forging cooperation in agricultural research at Indian training institutions and universities, besides encouraging commercial linkages.

Terrorism: India and the US established a Joint Working Group on countering terrorism in early 2000 which has been meeting regularly twice a year since then, alternately in Washington and New Delhi. Over a dozen meetings of the Group have been held so far. The Joint Working Group has proved to be a useful mechanism for exchange of information, intelligence sharing, anti-terrorism training programmes, etc., and for strengthening institutional links between crime prevention agencies in the two countries. The JWG also addresses itself to related areas of bioterrorism, aviation security, biometrics, cyber-security and terrorism, WMD-terrorism, terrorist finance and money laundering, and violent extremism.

People-to-people Relationships: Easily and often overlooked is the aspect of the India-US people-to-people network which exerts its own dynamics on the evolving bilateral relationship in the 21st century. Apart from the nearly 3-million strong community in the US, there are today over 65,000 Americans living and working in India, lured by its growing economy, available job opportunities, and the richness of its culture. The India Caucus is the largest in the US Congress dedicated to improving relations with any single country. And, more Indian students are studying in the US today than ever before—nearly 80,000, second only perhaps to China. The growth of the Indian student population in the US has been phenomenal, doubling in just five years. India is also the largest source of temporary workers into the US and the second largest source of legal migration to the US, behind Mexico.

Beyond outsourcing which often tends to become one of the favourite whipping boys of US politicians on hustings, it should be noted that no less than 34 global Indian companies have so far invested some $6 billion in the US through acquisitions and mergers and created 40,000 jobs in the process. Moreover as business has blossomed, India and the US hope to double by 2009 their two-way trade volume now touching almost $30 billion. This figure is not difficult to attain considering that in the coming years when the orders placed by Indian carriers for 138 planes from Boeing, including 37 of its latest offering, the Boeing 787 Dreamliner, fructify. And these figures do not even include big ticket items that never appear in trade statistics like the USS Trenton, the first warship India has ever acquired from the US.[38]

India-US civilian nuclear cooperation initiative: A word about the India-US civilian nuclear cooperation initiative which has become a major landmark in a key area of cooperation between India and the US. It was concluded in spite of the rough weather it encountered with India's opposition parties, especially the Left, who had even threatened to bring the then ruling minority government down in case the Government went ahead with signing the Agreement with the US. Defying all logic, this was an unbelievable case where the country's national interest was crassly suborned by partisan political interests, to the unbridled delight of both India's nuclear neighbours who could have hardly achieved themselves what India's opposition parties were obligingly doing for them. Both must have laughed all the way to nearest reactor! To add insult to injury, China reportedly offered Pakistan a similar deal to the one concluded between India and the US.

More to the point, however, the burgeoning India-US relationship could in any case not have been held hostage to a single issue. That relationship would have not only survived the civilian nuclear imbroglio but continued to thrive in spite of it because of the inexorable currents of the evolving geopolitical landscape that includes a perceptibly-shared, even if deliberately unstated, fear of a rapidly-resurgent China. Moreover, in that landscape, India and the US who are in the vanguard of democracy on the global stage and cherish similar values and ideology, will always find enough common ground that will keep them together to in the quest for freedom and human values.

In fact, a 16-country poll conducted by the Pew Research Centre in Washington in 2005 found that Indians harbour the most favourable image of the United States, more so than even Canadians or the British. According to the Survey, over 71 per cent Indians had a positive view of America—a figure up from 54 per cent only three years earlier. Whether it is in the corridors of power in New Delhi, or in the streets, the perception of the US in India has undergone a phenomenal change after the end of

---

38. Renamed as INS Jalashwa (Sea Hippopotamus) after being commissioned into the Indian Navy, it is expected to make a quantum jump in integral sealift and airlift capabilities of the Indian Navy.

the Cold War. Before that it aroused neutral feelings at best and hostility at worst, in part because of the USS Enterprise memories of 1971, but mostly because the US was seen as pathologically pro-Pakistan and anti-India, and the added "ganging-up" with China in 1971 invariably elicited epithets that could easily match those of the Nixon-Kissinger duo at the time.

The people-to-people factor has exerted its own dynamic in the past couple of decades when tens of thousands of migrating Indians achieved their dream of professional progress and financial prosperity in the United States. In recent years, with the removal of foreign exchange restrictions, Indian students have constituted the largest number of overseas students coming to study in American colleges. As more and more Indians travel to and from the United States for vacations, to visit family, or for business, there is greater appreciation for the American people and their open society. To quote Indian Prime Minister Manmohan Singh,[39] "As two great democracies we are natural partners in many ways. We are at a juncture in our history where we can embark on a partnership between India and the United States, a partnership that can draw both on principles as well as pragmatism".

Paul Wolfowitz, the former World Bank chief and a former US deputy defense secretary, apparently used to lament that India had for long been a "black hole" in calculations of the US foreign policy establishment in which sanctions were substituted for engagement.[40] Even before she became Secretary of State, Condoleezza Rice pointed out that "India is an element in China's calculation, and it should be in America's too. India is not a great power yet, but it has the potential to emerge as one."

The term 'strategic relationship' has been used to define the US-India relationship ever since the Bush visit. However, a bilateral relationship does not become a strategic one just by repeating the phrase several times over. Like any other relationship, it has to be carefully nurtured, tightened with appropriate nuts and bolts at the right places and suffused with a certain amount of concrete realism. Thus, when Pakistan was declared a so-called MNNA (Major Non-Nato Ally) after 9/11, surely the strategic partner ought to have been consulted. When India expressed its misgivings

---

39. PM Manmohan Singh's own daughter is a civil liberties and human rights lawyer in the US, whose professional work often brings her in conflict with government agencies and other US officialdom.

40. Strobe Talbott. *Engaging India—Diplomacy, Democracy & the Bomb*. 209.

about the action (given the history of Indo-Pak animosities and Pakistan's well known proclivity to use US supplied military equipment in conflicts with India), not only was she brushed aside but to add insult injury was told that India was welcome to join it too, if she wanted. This only brought back past nightmares of "hyphenation"—that India could be treated the same way as Pakistan. If there is one single issue that India always detested in its past relationship with the US, it was this US tendency to bracket India with Pakistan—a nation of 120 million *versus* a nation of 1 billion, a military dictatorship *versus* a flourishing democracy, a theocratic state *versus* a secular state, an epicentre of terrorism *versus* a victim of terrorism, and the list could go on and on. Nobody in India could ever fathom why all the concentrated intellectual capital at Foggy Bottom failed to discern these very basic and very obvious differences that was not exactly rocket science. Thus, the challenge before US leadership is to invest the 'strategic partnership' with concrete and meaningful elements, beyond the confines of mere rhetoric. Of course, equally the challenge before the Indian leadership is to forge a national consensus for a strategic partnership with the US without looking over their shoulders to see what the reaction of any third country would be. The only and ultimate yardstick for any measure in this regard has to be the national interest.

At the time of this writing, the US is close to approaching the final lap of electoral campaign that will determine the new Presidency in January 2009. Both the contenders—Republican John McCain and Democrat Barack Obama—have gone on record to express their commitment for strengthening ties with India, indicating that the emerging 'strategic partnership' enjoys bipartisan support. On the Indo-US Civilian Nuclear Agreement, while a McCain Presidency would naturally carry forward the Bush Agenda on this issue, even Obama has confirmed his support in the following words: "The existing nuclear agreement effectively balances a range of important issues—from America's strategic relationship with India to its non-proliferation concerns to India's energy needs. I am therefore reluctant to seek changes." When asked in what specific areas he would like to see US-India relations grow, his reply was, "Across-the-board would be the short answer."[41]

---

41.   http://www.rediff.com/news/2008/jul/11ndeal14.htm

2 | The India-China Relationship

SECTION I

THE PAST

China, that mighty country with a mighty past, our neighbor, has been our friend
through the ages and that friendship will endure and grow

Pandit Jawaharlal Nehru, 7 September 1946

For Mao, Nehru was "half man, half devil" and the task of communists was to
"wash off his face so that it won't be frightening, like a devil's."

Record of Conversation of Mao Zedong with
Representatives of Socialist Countries, Moscow, 1959

In the Spring of 1945, Mao Zedong, who was then only the Chairman of the Chinese Communist Party, expressed the hope that Britain would grant Independence to India once WWII was over because in his words "an independent and democratic India is not only the demand of the Indian people, but also a necessity for world peace."

Two years later, when India actually got her Independence from Britain after two centuries of colonial subjugation and at least a century's bitter struggle, he agreed with Stalin's assessment that grant of independence to India was a clever trick designed to preserve British investments and influence, and to perpetuate British economic control by conceding a meaningless political freedom.

Though the course of events may have been somewhat different, China too, after a century of humiliation at the hand of several European colonial powers, and a protracted civil war, became an independent Peoples' Republic in 1949. Both countries, thus, shared the common legacy of a troubled recent colonial past.

Pandit Nehru, India's first Prime Minister had a rather idealistic vision of the role that India and China—the world's oldest civilisations—would play in the emerging post WWII order. This new order that he dreamt of was to be based not on military strength, or upon power politics, but grounded in moral values—values that Buddha and Confucius and Mencius and Dao had bequeathed to millions of their own and succeeding generations throughout the vast Asian landmass. One of its keys was to be Afro-Asian solidarity and decolonisation, in which he saw China to be major player along with India. It was in this spirit that India extended a hand of friendship to China, becoming one of the earliest countries—indeed the second in the non-socialist world and the first in South Asia—to recognise the newly-established Republic.[1] In fact, the quest for a close friendship with China was one of the reasons that India had stayed out of the power blocs that emerged in the Cold War, preferring non-alignment instead. High level visits between leaders of both countries took place in 1954.[2]

With the help of hindsight—which is always 20/20—we now know that the Chinese worldview was quite different. The new Communist regime was downright pragmatic in its approach to world politics, rooted firmly in what political scientists call the "realist" school, unlike Nehru's starry-eyed approach which epitomised the best traditions of the "idealist" school. Accordingly, soon after coming to power, the new communist regime in Peking proceeded to consolidate its hold over far-flung areas which were once part of the Chinese empire. The first of these was Tibet. According to the Chinese, they "invited" Tibetans early in the 1950s to "accede peacefully" to China, backing up the plea quite unambiguously by stationing an army near the city of Chamdo in East Tibet. An anxious Tibetan delegation rushed to Beijing to talk to the Chinese government in an effort to defuse tensions and to prevent the invasion, but such was China's hurry that on 7 October 1950, the day the Tibetan delegation was scheduled to arrive in Peking, 80,000 PLA soldiers marched into Tibet and announced its "peaceful liberation", what else?

Soon afterwards, on May 23, 1951, Tibet's spiritual leader and most revered personage, His Holiness the Dalai Lama, was forced to sign

---

1.   India and China established full diplomatic relations on 1 April, 1950.

2.   Premier Zhou Enlai visited India in June 1954. Prime Minister Nehru visited China in October 1954.

under duress, the "17-Point Agreement" surrendering to China. Forced upon the Tibetan government and people at gunpoint, the so-called "Agreement",[3] the PRC claims, shows that Tibetans not only agreed to, but actually invited Chinese Communist troops to "liberate" Tibet![4] The Chinese promised to leave Tibet's political system unaltered, to uphold the status, functions and powers of the Dalai Lama, and the preservation of the religious beliefs, customs and traditions of the Tibetan people, including the Lamaist monasteries. Each one of these so-called promises was subsequently honoured only in their breach. This, of course, begs the question as to why India did not do more to help. After all it did not require a stroke of extraordinary geopolitical genius to see that Tibet's continuation as a buffer state was as much in independent India's interest as it was in British India's interest. Partly, of course, it was a reluctant acceptance of the inevitable and unavoidable—arising from the fact that India just simply did not have the military capability to enforce an outcome that she would have ideally desired. In part, it was also because India did want to be seen holding on to the extraterritorial rights acquired by India's erstwhile British rulers in Tibet.[5] Most of all, though, it was because of Pandit Nehru's romantic vision of a future of Asia built on the foundation of a new partnership between the two oldest world civilisations—India and China. If the unavoidable price for that had to be paid by relinquishing all rights inherited by the successor state from the British, then Nehru figured, so be it.

Tibet had been independent since 1914, and China's hold over it even before that was tenuous at best—depending on how powerful the government in China happened to be at any particular time. Even then, with Tibetans paying 'tribute' to the Emperor in Beijing (in cash or gifts) it was a case of China exercising "suzerainty" at best, not "sovereignty" as she claims. In fact as late as September 1946, as Vice President of the Interim Government, Pandit Nehru had convened an Afro-Asian Conference in New Delhi where a Tibetan delegate was seated, as was a representative from China.

---

3. The Agreement offered Tibet "Regional autonomy under the unified leadership of the Central Peoples' Government".

4. The Chinese official press spoke of the need to "liberate Tibet from Anglo-American imperialists and their running dog Nehru".

5. The Younghusband Expedition of 1903-04.

In the event, India was unable to stop the Chinese invasion and sought only assurances of cultural and religious autonomy for Tibet. The Chinese readily provided such assurances in the ensuing Agreement that the two countries signed in 1954, which implicitly recognised China's control over Tibet. India's hopes were soon belied, as China not only increased its repression of the gentle Tibetan people but also began to systematically destroy their religion and culture. When that was not found to work, China sought to bring about a change in the demographics of Tibet by populating it with Han Chinese so that native Tibetans became a minority in their own land. The result was that revolts against Chinese occupation erupted in several parts of Tibet, only to be suppressed with increasing brutality. The continued and relentless repression of Tibetans, and with serious fears for his own life, eventually led to His Holiness the Dalai Lama fleeing to India in 1959 with some twenty thousand of his followers in search of political asylum. This was naturally granted, and he set up his Headquarters[6] in Dharamsala in the state of Himachal Pradesh. This greatly upset the Chinese government despite Indian assurances that he would not be allowed to use Indian soil to carry on political activities against China. As is well known, the Dalai Lama, ever since then, has been pleading the cause of Tibet in chancelleries around the world, albeit with limited success. He is graciously received by politicians, statesmen and leaders around the world—all of whom are sympathetic to his cause but have little leverage in the matter except for moral suasion to urge Beijing to leave the Tibetans free to practice their religion and nurture their culture and traditions.

Unbeknownst to India until many years later (1957), the Chinese had started building a road (Highway G219) linking Tibet with the equally restive province of Sinkiang, through the Indian state of Jammu & Kashmir in the early 1950s. Although the area was clearly demarcated in maps, it was not regularly patrolled, being a high and barren plateau. When India took up the matter with China, the latter questioned the validity of the McMahon Line, the border demarcated by British Surveyor, Sir Henry McMahon on the basis of the 'watershed' principle, between British India and Tibet in the 1914. Of course the Chinese had a perfectly valid

---

6.   Often referred to in common parlance as the Tibetan "Government-in-Exile", a term that India officially discourages in order not to offend the sensitivities of the Chinese.

argument in as much as that they were never stopped when the road was being constructed, and if it was through Indian territory as India claimed, then surely should they not have been stopped in their tracks? Since the road cuts through a swathe of territory that is part of the state of Jammu & Kashmir, the entire area to the east of it and covering some 30,000 sq.kms, known as the Aksai Chin plateau, is under *de facto* Chinese occupation until today.

Meanwhile, after consolidating their hold over Tibet, in the 1950s, the Chinese also started several probing missions elsewhere on the India Tibet border. Since the border was clearly demarcated during British times, India sent out patrols to interdict the Chinese probing missions. Several clashes occurred throughout the 1950s, some of them fairly serious. Whenever a protest was lodged by India, the Chinese response invariably would be that the new government in Beijing had not had enough time to study the old maps. As it turned out later, this was a consummate ploy to buy time, probe India's defences along the Tibet border and generally to gauge both India's political will and military capability to take on the Chinese. Increasing skirmishes led to talks between Pandit Nehru and Premier Zhou Enlai in 1959. The talks were inconclusive, and with the situation along the border deteriorating further, an armed clash ensued in October 1962. The well-prepared PLA inflicted a decisive defeat on the ill-prepared Indian forces, who were clearly taken by surprise and suffered substantial casualties. China held all the territory she claimed and the hitherto sacrosanct McMahon line lay in tatters. The new line was christened the "Line of Actual Control" subject to a final settlement of the border between India and China. Over the years, China has added the entire Indian province of Arunachal Pradesh in India's north-east to its list of claims over India in the area. It my be noteworthy to mention here that while China does not recognise the McMahon line as demarcating the Indo-Tibetan border, they do indeed accept it as the boundary marker with Nepal and Burma in the same region.

To sum up, current Chinese claims on Indian territory, arising out of its occupation of Tibet, are as follows:

1. The Western sector: 30,000 sq. km of high plateau country known as the Aksai Chin in the Ladakh district of the Indian state of Jammu &

Kashmir bordering Tibet and the Xinjiang province of China, through which a road was built.

2. The Middle sector: 20,000 sq. km on either side of the Himalayan watershed and passes (in the states of Uttar Pradesh, Himachal Pradesh and Sikkim).

3. The Eastern sector: 90,000 sq. km comprising the entire Indian province of Arunachal Pradesh (formerly known as NEFA or the North-East Frontier Agency).

Of course, all these claims arose after China's forcible occupation of Tibet in 1950. No Tibetan government had ever made any such claims on India.

China's successful nuclear tests in the atmosphere in 1964, coming so soon after India's military defeat at her hands (1962) raised alarm bells in India. India informally sought a nuclear "umbrella" from several existing nuclear powers, which was simply not forthcoming. I mention this because it could well have been a contributing factor to the rationale for India's own quest for a nuclear weapon that led to the nuclear tests the so called "PNE"—the Peaceful Nuclear Explosion—twelve years later (1974). It was given this name not because any nuclear explosion is *per se* 'peaceful', but simply because it was not a weapons test but strictly a technology-demonstrator, and India made it amply clear that it had no intention of proceeding ahead with the option to develop nuclear weapons. As is known now, this self-restraint lasted for another quarter of a century.

Meanwhile, a parallel development that severely impacted India-China relations was the 'all-weather friendship' that suddenly blossomed between China and Pakistan after the 1962 India-China border war, duly and properly anchored in the timeless principle of one's enemy's enemy being a friend. This was in spite of Pakistan being a staunch ally of the US and firmly committed to halt the spread of communism spearheaded in Asia by the Chinese communists. Hence, the membership of Baghdad, SEATO and CENTO and the generous arms transfers by the US to Pakistan in terms of these pacts. And yet Pakistan was now warming up to a nation it was supposed to "contain" under these pacts. For Chinese foreign policy, this must undoubtedly have been an unexpected but wholly welcome 'coup', for which Pakistan was amply rewarded in the years to come.

These rewards were plentiful, unprecedented and entirely at India's expense. They began with moral and diplomatic, if not much material, assistance to Pakistan in the 1965 war with India. More of the same in the 1971 war that led to the emergence of Bangladesh. But very much more significantly it came by way of help in the ensuing years to build up Pakistan's nuclear weapons capability—thereby saving Bhutto and his Pakistani citizenry from having to eat grass.[7] Further help by way of delivery systems for Pakistan's nuclear weapons was facilitated by Beijing through the North Koreans who supplied the necessary missiles.[8] Needless to add, China has been a signatory to the NPT ever since its inception in 1968.

In terms of the India-US-China triangle, there are a few noteworthy pointers relating to this period that must be borne in mind. The US never recognised the communist government that took power in Beijing in 1949, reserving that honour for the KMT-led Chiang Kai-shek government that had fled to Taiwan after losing to the Communists in the Chinese civil war that ended in 1949. Even the UN seat, including the prestigious veto-wielding permanent membership of the Security Council was occupied by the KMT. Without going into the origins of this story, suffice it to say that during the Chinese civil war (1945-1949), the US was supporting Chiang Kai-shek's KMT Party, while the Soviets were helping the Chinese Communist Party (CCP) led by Mao Zedong. Once the CCP emerged victorious and took over the reigns of power in Beijing, the US held on to the belief that Chiang Kai-shek's KMT enjoyed enough popular support on the mainland to enable it to retake power at an appropriate time. Even as this belief turned into a myth, the US was unwilling to recognise the ground realities and all through the 1950s, 60s and until the early 70s, it kept supporting Taiwan's claim to be the real representative of China. India, on the other hand, having recognised the communist government in 1949 itself, pressed repeatedly, in and outside the UN, for China to be admitted to UN membership. This did not please US in the middle of a raging Cold War in which the containment of communist China and the

---

7. Reacting to India's 1974 PNE, Zulfiqar Ali Bhutto famously declared "even if Pakistanis have to eat grass we will make the bomb".

8. In June 1999, India intercepted a Korean freighter off the Gujarat Coast which was carrying missile parts intended for Pakistan. The cargo was seized and intelligence shared by India with the US.

Soviet Union was the centrepiece of its world outlook and foreign policy. It is an interesting quirk of international politics that for nearly a quarter of a century India vigorously espoused the cause of China's admission to the UN when it meant taking up cudgels with US on the issue. Once the US permitted China to join, almost the first action in the triangle was the US instigation to China to attack India, and then years later the US and China working together to keep India out of the UN Security Council (as a Permanent Member). After Pokharan II, both the US and China censured India. One action by President Clinton that really riled India was an unwarranted reference to India's nuclear tests during his visit to China in June 1998 when a Joint US-China statement called upon India to stop any further nuclear tests and to sign the CTBT "immediately and unconditionally." India did not expect the US to join hands with China and gang up against India on Chinese soil. Observers in India also did not fail to note that Clinton failed to make any mention of China's transfer of nuclear materials and technology to Pakistan which, together with China's N-stockpile and menacing behaviour towards India was what was responsible for India's decision to go nuclear.

This chapter would not be complete without the mention, significantly, of the publication of a 1954 map by the communist regime showing former "tributary areas of the Manchu Empire" that were described as "having been lost to Foreign Powers" since then.[9] As it was during the Manchu Empire that foreign incursions (mostly by European powers and Japan) into China began, the implication is loud and clear, namely that China has every right—whether pressed to claim or not—over these territories. This map would send shudders down the spines of many South Asian, SE Asian and East Asian countries today and perhaps explain the extreme wariness with which these countries perceive China and look to regional powers like India, Australia and Japan, and the sole extra-regional (super) power to provide a counterbalance. This map includes not only all the Himalayan nations of Nepal, Sikkim, and Bhutan but also the entire Indian state of Arunachal Pradesh, large swathes of Assam (India), besides the whole of Burma, Thailand, Laos, Cambodia, Vietnam, the Sulu Archipelago, Taiwan, Japan's Ryukyu Islands, Korea (North and South), Mongolia and large swathes of the Russian Far East up to and including Sakhalin Island. (See Map...)

---

9. By the same token, India could lay claim to Indochina and Bali in Indonesia, which were part of the Mauryan and Chola kingdoms in the 11th and 12th century AD.

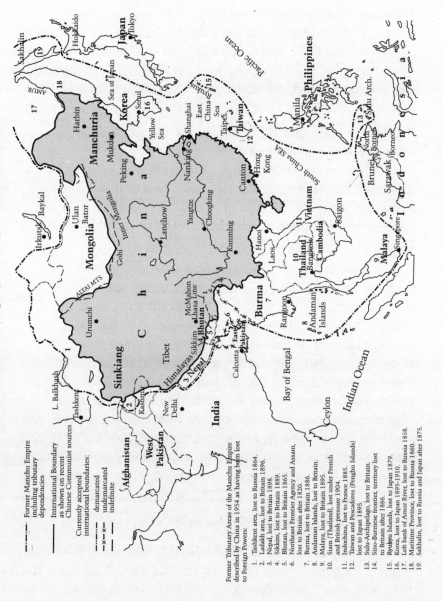

The Manchu Empire, Chinese Communist Version

Former Manchu Empire including tributary dependencies

International Boundary as shown on recent Chinese Communist sources

Currently accepted international boundaries:
demarcated
undemarcated
indefinite

Former Tributary Areas of the Manchu Empire described by China in 1954 as having been lost to Foreign Powers:

1. Tashkent area, lost to Russia 1864.
2. Ladakh area, lost to Britain 1896.
3. Nepal, lost to Britain 1898.
4. Sikkim, lost to Britain 1889.
5. Bhutan, lost to Britain 1865.
6. Northeast Frontier Agency and Assam, lost to Britain after 1820.
7. Burma, lost to Britain 1886.
8. Andaman Islands, lost to Britain.
9. Malaya, lost to Britain 1895.
10. Siam (Thailand), lost under French and British pressure 1904.
11. Indochina, lost to France 1885.
12. Taiwan and Pescadores (Penghu Islands) lost to Japan 1895.
13. Sulu-Archipelago, lost to Britain.
14. Sino-Burmese frontier, territory lost to Britain after 1886.
15. Ryukyu Islands, lost to Japan 1879.
16. Korea, lost to Japan 1895–1910.
17. Left bank of Amur River, lost to Russia 1858.
18. Maritime Province, lost to Russia 1860.
19. Sakhalin, lost to Russia and Japan after 1875.

The annotation to the map refers to Nepal, Sikkim, Bhutan, Burma, Ladakh, NEFA (Arunachal Pradesh), Assam, Malaya and the Andaman Islands and the Sulu Archipelago as having been "lost" to Britain in the 1890s, the Tashkent area (modern day Uzbekistan), left bank of the Amur River, the Maritime Province and Sakhalin having been "lost" to Russia in the years between the 1850s-1870s, and the Pescadores, Ryukyu and Korea having been "lost" to Japan in the 1870s-1890s. Similarly, Thailand was supposedly "lost" under French and British pressure in 1904, and Indochina "lost" to the French in 1885.

Interestingly though, superimposed on the same map is another boundary showing China's current claims which, while mercifully excluding from its ambit Burma, Thailand, Malaysia, the Indochina countries, Koreas, Outer Mongolia and Russia, still includes parts of Burma, the entire Indian state of Arunachal Pradesh, parts of the Indian states of Uttar Pradesh and Himachal Pradesh and the whole of Aksai Chin, east of Highway G219 in Ladakh (J&K).

During the 1950s, the question of these maps often formed the subject matter of discussions between India and Chinese officials because it was observed that China was following a policy—deliberate or otherwise—which tended to follow the claims made in similar maps of that time. The matter was even taken up at the highest levels between Prime Minister Nehru and Premier Zhou Enlai. The uniform response to all these concerns invariably was that these were 'old' Chinese maps of previous regimes that the new (communist) government had had no time to revise since assuming power. This explanation was obviously accepted hook, line and sinker by the then leadership, thereby inducing a false sense of complacency, leading to a perilous situation after 1959 and culminating in national grief three years later.

SECTION II

CHALLENGES AND OPPORTUNITIES

Diplomatic relations at the Ambassadorial level, broken off at the height of the border war in 1962, were restored between India and China in 1976, soon after Mao's death. The world's two largest nations appeared to have realised the need to restore a semblance of normalcy in their bilateral relationship. The Cultural Revolution in China was now over, the country was trying hard to shake-off its image of an international pariah and to occupy its rightful place in the comity of nations, having been admitted to the UN in 1972, and the era of reforms under Deng Xiaoping had begun. The time had therefore come to normalise relations with two of its largest neighbours—of which India was one. In 1974, India successfully tested a nuclear device, and even though it was not a 'nuclear bomb' *per se*, the point would hardly have been missed by a politically-astute Chinese leadership. The so-called Cold War was beginning to look somewhat meaningless, what with China and the US being equidistant from, if not actually equally hostile towards, the Soviet Union. And what of Pakistan—the US ally in the frontline of the effort to contain Chinese communism—now having brokered the deal that actually brought the US and China together? In this topsy-turvy world of shifting alignments, national interest had far overtaken any ideological considerations. China was even beginning to look favourably at the capitalist model for certain aspects of its long-stifled economic development in which the profit motive or 'becoming rich' was no longer a dirty, anti-revolutionary concept. It was the same pragmatism that dictated a normalisation of relations with India. After all you cannot be a 'great' nation if you are at war in your immediate neighbourhood with two of your largest neighbours.

A change of government in New Delhi helped matters along. In 1979, India's External Affairs Minister Atal Bihari Vajpayee, paid an ice-breaking visit to China, the first such high-ranking visit after the 1962 war. The visit was largely symbolic, and indeed had to be cut short due to China's attack on Vietnam ("teaching a lesson" as Deng Xiaoping called it) at the time of the visit. The previous such "lesson" China had taught was to India!

In 1981, Chinese Foreign Minister, Huang Hua, paid a return visit to India, and it was decided to resume the discussions on the vexed border question that had led to the 1962 war. Five rounds of border talks ensued in the coming years, when Mrs. Indira Gandhi was the Prime Minister[10] but without any tangible outcome. Bilateral relations got a slight jolt in 1987 when India granted full statehood to Arunachal Pradesh—which China claims as part of its territory. In a show of its disapproval, the Chinese PLA advanced menacingly into the adjacent Sumdorong Chu Valley but later withdrew when challenged.

---

10. Her second innings as Prime Minister (1980-1984).

In December 1988, Prime Minister Rajiv Gandhi paid a visit to China which set the tone for positive "atmospheric changes" in bilateral relations. Both sides agreed to break the impasse on the boundary question and to maintain peace and stability along the Line of Actual Control (LAC). An agreement was signed to set up a Joint Working Group to defuse tension along the border. More important, both countries agreed that the border question would not be permitted to hold hostage cooperation in other areas of mutual benefit. In that spirit, several agreements on cooperation in Science and Technology, as well as educational and cultural exchange programmes etc., were concluded.

Premier Li Peng paid a return visit to India in December 1991, during which he and PM Narasimha Rao reiterated that the border issue would not be allowed to obstruct cooperation in other areas of mutual interest. A Trade Protocol was signed to promote bilateral border trade. Later, a visit to Beijing by Prime Minister Rao in September 1993 led to the conclusion of an agreement to "maintain peace and tranquility" along the LAC.

With continuing improvement, the level of bilateral exchanges was further upgraded with President Jiang Zemin's visit to India in November 1996. Four new agreements were signed during this visit including, most significantly one relating to the implementation of confidence building measures (CBMs) along the border areas, including, notably, the downsizing respective military forces along the LAC. The resultant reduction of tension along the border was seen as a "major breakthrough" in Sino-Indian bilateral relations.

India's nuclear tests in May 1998 aroused Chinese criticism, which was mild at first. What greatly annoyed China was her being cited as one of the main reasons for India exercising her nuclear option after a quarter of a century of self-imposed restraint following the PNE of 1974. Prime Minister Vajpayee's letter to President Clinton, deliberately leaked by the White House to the US press, accused China of posing a "nuclear threat" to India. India's Defence Minister, George Fernandez had said so in as many words earlier, leaving no doubt that unlike Pakistan's tit-for-tat nuclear tests two weeks later which were "India-specific", India's decision hinged around nuclear threats from both the West (Pakistan) as well as the East (China). What was left unsaid, of course, was that China (an NPT signatory) was solely responsible for aiding and abetting in the acquisition of nuclear weapons by Pakistan.

The Chinese government brushed aside the Indian accusations as "utterly groundless". The immediate fallout was that China cancelled its decision to participate in the pre-scheduled 1998 meeting of the Joint Working Group (JWG) on the Border, alternatively held in each country, to discuss further CBMs (confidence-building measures).

Once again, both countries moved quickly to get relations back on track. External Affairs Minister Jaswant Singh visited China (June 1999) to reassure Chinese leaders that India perceived no threat from China. Within a few months, the JWG process was resumed and in April 2000 India participated in the first ever   bilateral Security Dialogue held in Beijing. The discussions covered issues of global and regional security, based on the premise that as two major Asian countries, they bore an important responsibility for maintenance of regional peace and stability. Premier Zhu Rongji visited India in 2002.

In 2003, Prime Minister Vajpayee visited China. In 2005 Premier Wen Jiabao reciprocated with a visit to India. President Hu Jintao visited India in 2006. The same year (July 2006), the historic silk road passing through Nathu La in Sikkim was reopened and border trade resumed. Trade between India and China reached $18.7 billion in 2007 year, making her India's 2nd largest trading partner after the US.

Nearly 10 meetings of the JWGs (set up in 1993 and 1996) have taken place since then, albeit with little progress. However neither side wishes to disturb the status quo.

2006 was celebrated as the India-China Friendship Year with exchanges of high-level visits from both countries and the signing of an MoU between the two Defence Ministries. Economic relations received a shot in the arm with the opening of border trade through the Nathu La border pass in mid-2006 and a high-level business seminar in India and China jointly organised by FICCI/CII[11] from the Indian side and CCPIT[12] from the Chinese side. An MoU was also signed on cooperation in S&T.

---

11   FICCI: Federation of Indian Chambers of Commerce and Industry (Based in New Delhi); CII: Confederation of Indian Industry (Based in New Delhi).

12.   CCPIT: China Council for the promotion of International Trade (Based in Beijing).

On the cultural front, a Cultural Exchange Programme was signed, an Indian-style Buddhist Temple inaugurated in Luoyang, and a Xuan Zang Memorial set up in Nalanda. Also on the anvil is an exhibition titled "Journey of Buddhism from India to China", and the participation of Peking Opera Troupe in India's National Opera Festival. A TV documentary series named "Along the Footprints of Xuan Zang" will be produced by China's Central TV (CCTV).

Prime Minister Manmohan Singh visited China in January 2008. The talks were reported to have been held in an 'atmosphere of sincerity, warmth and friendship' and were described as 'constructive and forward looking', resulting in the signing of a grand-sounding document titled a 'Shared Vision' for the 21st Century.

In all, some 11 agreements were signed—in economic planning, housing, health and culture and land management etc. With bilateral trade having reached $30 billion in 2007, Singh and Wen decided to raise the target from $40 billion by 2010 to $60 billion, and ordered the launch of a 'Feasibility Study' for the possible setting up of a future Regional Trading Arrangement involving India and China.

While these external manifestations of seemingly normal, indeed overtly friendly, relations continue, the internal realities should not be lost sight of. This is the biggest challenge that faces India in its relations with China in the foreseeable future, because core differences remain unresolved. India needs to shake itself out of a self-serving delusion that these growing economic ties and cultural exchanges will *ipso facto* lead to a resolution of key outstanding issues. The sooner India's political leadership wakes up to the geopolitical realities of China's long-term aims in the region, the less will be the chances of a 1962-type national disappointment and breast beating. That time too, in spite of repeated border skirmishes—some minor, others not so—and Chinese maps that kept showing large chunks of Indian territory as parts of China, India was caught totally unprepared and suffered a humiliating defeat. Then, the blame was squarely laid at the door of an unrepentant fellow-traveller who was the highest ranking civilian in charge of India's defences. But India circa 2008 is not India circa 1962. And 46 years is a long time to learn a simple lesson of history. Today, the people of India will not be as forgiving of the political leadership if it fails to takes timely measures to get relations with China on a realistic track without leaving it to the next generation to sort out. It must be remembered that China can afford to be smug and take its own time because it has all the chips conveniently stacked in its favour. The time to 'react' is over; India needs to be proactive in sorting out the outstanding issues rather than let 'time' sort them out.

Let us face the facts squarely. Eleven rounds of border negotiations, started with great fanfare in 1988 have yielded little beyond establishing "peace & tranquility" along the disputed border, and ritualistic reiterations to resolve the outstanding issues in a spirit of mutual accommodation. China has nothing to lose but everything to gain by dragging its feet over the issue. After all it is sitting pretty over 30,000 sq. km in Aksai Chin and 20,000 sq. km elsewhere along the border from where it can never be dislodged. Conversely, India has everything to lose by not pressing for an early resolution of the boundary issue. But China will not negotiate unless it becomes, or more correctly, is made aware that it has a price to pay for dragging its feet on the issue. After all, with regional and global ambitions to power and glory, China cannot be seen to be at odds with her neighbours in her own backyard, so it suits her to carry on the pretension that everything is fine while she is in complete command of the situation. As it is, China has succeeded in ensuring that India negotiates with her always from a position of weakness, as a supplicant, not as an equal, much like the proverbial skinny kid in a schoolyard asking the school bully to return the marbles that he has snatched away from him.

What are India's options, one may ask, if all the chips are stacked in China's favour? There are many, but India has to get its act—or political will—together to exercise them in a manner designed to bring about a favourable outcome for itself.

On the crucial border issue, India has to play the Tibet card more deftly. After all, before 1949, India never had a border with China. It was only after China's invasion and ruthless occupation of the country by force soon after 1949 that India suddenly found the Tibetan 'buffer' disappear overnight, replaced by a giant nation on its doorstep. The US was too busy with the reconstruction of post-war Europe and the emerging crisis in the Korean peninsula to pay much heed to events in Tibet. The only country that had a vital interest in preserving the 'buffer' status of Tibet was India. For various reasons India could do nothing about it on its own, and was too loud a protagonist of the policy of nonalignment to seek help from the Western powers.[13] India's 1954 Agreement with China virtually recognised China's sovereignty over Tibet without India asking for anything in return except the preservation of Tibet's religious and cultural autonomy. It is pertinent to note here that no Tibetan government had ever made any claims on Indian territory that China made after its occupation of Tibet—and substantially achieved after 1962—in Aksai Chin and elsewhere, including Arunachal Pradesh. Even the recognition of Sikkim's accession to India (1975) has been accepted by China with great reluctance, and made to appear as a major concession that it was making to India. Surely, isn't there a price that India should be demanding for her unhesitating recognition of China's absorption of Tibet? After all the Dalai Lama fled to India when China began systematic repression of the people and the cultural-religious institutions of Tibet, in violation of the terms of the 1954 understanding with India. Why, then, should India bend over backwards to please China as it did during the recent worldwide protests that accompanied the Olympic torch by being overenthusiastic about preventing genuine protest during the torch's passage through India? When will India understand that such acts of appeasement are interpreted by China as signs of weakness? The challenge therefore, before India's policy makers is to let China know that in return for her acceptance of China's sovereignty over Tibet, the border problem needs to be resolved to India's satisfaction, the so-called 'claims' over Arunachal Pradesh dropped and the Tibetans' right to practice their religion and uphold their culture and traditions be respected. After all, today even the Dalai Lama no longer seeks an Independent Tibet; all he wants, too, is simply for China to respect Tibet's religious-cultural autonomy.

The next challenge before India's policymakers is to get out of the shackles of containment that China has so successfully confined India to. Even if we leave out the "all-weather" friendship with Pakistan, from Nepal to Bangladesh, and from Sri Lanka to Myanmar, China has

---

13.   In an internal Government memo, Pandit Nehru wrote to Home Minister Sardar Patel (November 18, 1950) as follows: "We cannot save Tibet, as we should have liked to do, and our very attempt to save it might well bring greater trouble to it. It would be unfair to Tibet for us to bring this trouble upon her without having the capacity to help her effectively. It may be possible, however, that we might be able to help Tibet to retain a large measure of her autonomy."

systematically edged India out of its own natural sphere of influence—in part by appearing to act as a 'big brother' vis-à-vis their relations with India. SAARC was the institution designed to counter this. It has failed in this task, partly because India has not put in enough effort to forge a united regional identity among its member nations, and partly because they do not see themselves as stakeholders of any substance. SAARC has not succeeded in emulating ASEAN and later India, perhaps out of a sense of some frustration, began diverting its energies in BIMST-EC and MGC, albeit without concomitant results. China's only aim in cultivating these countries is to cut India down to size—an aim which she has pursued with incredible tenacity and achieved remarkable success. Pakistan, of course, was an exceptional case for that country would have been "eating grass" today if it wasn't for China's nuclear largesse; and that is only the tip of the iceberg of Chinese help which spans the entire gamut from military hardware (including missile delivery systems, brokered through North Korea) to economic assistance. Nepal was quick to seek 'equidistance' from India and China after 1962 and emboldened enough by friendship with China to challenge India's influence in the Kingdom—which will stand further diluted now with Maoists having come to power in Nepal. With Myanmar, China was quick to seize the opportunity to cozy up to a military junta despised by the West and for long shunned by an India that was keen to see democracy restored after Aung San Suu Kyi won the elections. It paid handsome dividends. China was permitted by the junta to set up naval facilities in the Cocos Islands on the northern tip of India's Andaman and Nicobar Island chain in the Bay of Bengal, a striking distance from the Headquarters of FORTRAN, India's only integrated strategic joint Army-Navy-Air Force command guarding the vital sea lanes at the head of the Straits of Malacca. China also succeeded in persuading the junta to abandon a deal with India to supply gas and divert it at the last moment to China instead.

Having bottled up India in the Bay of Bengal through naval facilities in the Cocos Islands to the east, China is poised to repeat the performance on the west through facilities at the Pakistani port of Gwadar in Baluchistan which is being built with active Chinese assistance. Add to this the military superiority of the Chinese Army in Tibet (as compared to on the Indian side), buttressed by excellent logistics thanks to the

Qinghai-Tibet rail link completed recently and the presence of 66 nuclear-capable ballistic missiles in Tibet[14] targeted at India capable of reaching every major city, one can see how effectively China has "bottled-up" India. The military portion of this challenge can only be met by India's strategic planners. However, the political challenge can be met by taking a leaf out of China's own book, by doing what she did after the serious clashes in the Spring of 1969 with the Soviet forces in the Ussuri River sector of their common border.

What China did then, and what India ought to do now, is to seriously contemplate how best to offset this threat from China by leveraging relationships. In the Cold War era, something like the 1971 Indo-Soviet Treaty was sufficient to take care of the then imminent threat arising out of 'Washington-Islamabad-Peking Axis' directed against India. The present threat arising out of China's actions is not immediate in that sense, but is still clearly directed at the aim of not ceding any strategic space to India in Asia, much less on the global stage, under any circumstances. In other words, without saying so, China wants to be the undisputed regional hegemon in Asia, and since India is the only country—remotely or conceivably—capable of challenging that hegemony, China will do everything in its power to put her down, indeed keep her down, indefinitely. That explains the periodic threats over Arunachal Pradesh, backtracking on Sikkim, checkmating India's influence in her own neighbourhood, building "string of pearls" type bases around India, encouraging secessionist insurgencies in India's vulnerable North-east, prevaricating or procrastinating on the border issue under the convenient umbrella of the JWGs, of preventing India's permanent membership of the UN Security Council[15] etc. The list can go on and on. As if to compensate for this incontrovertible 'strategic containment', China goes on tactical overdrive to project a picture of reasonableness and bonhomie in bilateral

---

14. *China & India—Cooperation or Conflict* by WPS Sidhu and Jingdong Yuan. pp.51-53. If correct, then three-quarters of China's total inventory of medium and intermediate range n-capable missiles are targeted at India.

15. External Affairs Minister Pranab Mukherjee claimed in November 2006 that Chinese President Hu Jintao had "reiterated" Beijing's support for India's inclusion as a permanent member of the UNSC, but at a BRIC Foreign Minister's meeting in Yekaterinaburg in June 2008, the Chinese categorically refused to endorse a Russian proposal to the effect. Interestingly, in 1955, Pt. Nehru declined an offer for a permanent seat at the UNSC, stating that it should rightfully go to China.

cultural, economic and commercial exchanges and 'people-to-people' contacts in which "friends" of China in India are feted and lionised, and much brouhaha is made of the world's two most ancient civilisations whose stable ties will be a boon to the whole world!

It is not only the UN Security Council that China wants to keep India out of. China has equally robustly opposed India's membership in any meaningful Asian security architecture. It blocked India in the ASEAN+3, and has restricted India's presence in the SCO to merely being an observer, with slim hopes of ever becoming a member. And yet China protested loudly against India's 2007 Malabar series of naval exercises with the US which included, for the first time, Japan and Australia as well.

There have been repeated reports in the Indian press since late 2006 of Chinese probing missions and incursions in the so-called Finger Area of Sikkim that have become alarmingly frequent. In the last three years, close to 400 incidents of Chinese incursions along the border have taken place,[16] including 90 incidents so far in 2008. In April 2008, Chinese troops came 12 kms inside Arunachal Pradesh. In May 2008, a PLA patrol reportedly took up firing positions at an Indian border patrol in Demchok, northeast of Ladakh clearly on the Indian side of the LAC. So much for the fiction of "maintaining peace & tranquility along the border" or the concomitant understanding of not engaging one another even if accidental proximity occurs during patrolling along the border.[17]

When Chinese President Hu Jintao visited India in 2006, Prime Minister Manmohan Singh said there was "enough space for the two countries to develop together in a mutually supportive manner for mutual benefit". Such rhetoric makes for good bonhomie in banquet speeches during state visits by VIPs, but is not a substitute for a pragmatic policy. This is where India needs to carefully leverage her relationships—through stronger strategic partnerships with the US, with the EU and others—in areas ranging from economics and trade to military and security, from cultural linkages to involving the Indian diaspora, maximising the benefits of India's 'soft power'. India must remember that it has a distinct advantage over China when it comes to democracy and human rights—

---

16. Till June 2008.
17. *India Today*, 23 June 2008, pp.30-32.

dividends that are capable of translating into national advantage on the international arena. After all, the question on the world's lips invariably is "Will China's rise be peaceful?" Nobody, no country, ever surmises: "Will India's rise be peaceful?" Because it is taken for granted and is a question that never needs to be asked. But more of that later.

Suffice it to say for now, that that is perhaps the strongest lever in itself!

SECTION III

THE WAY AHEAD

Clearly, India and China have come a long way since the war of 1962. Both countries have succeeded in burying some of the ghosts of the past. Even though the border problem looms large in the bilateral relationship, it has been, for the time being at least, relegated to the background on pragmatic considerations by leaders of both countries, while putting in place a series of confidence-building measures (CBMs) that will obviate any precipitate clashes along the border. An incredible boost to the bilateral relationship has come in the form of increasing bilateral trade and lately even some FDI. At this rate, China is expected to replace the US as India's leading trading partner sooner than later. These developments augur well for the future of India-China relations.

The border problem—intractable as it appears to be—is something that will always loom in the background till it is resolved. The same of course is true about China's refusal to recognise Arunachal Pradesh as part of India. With the improved atmosphere in bilateral relations, these issues will have be resolved in due course, with give-and-take on both sides. They cannot be brushed under the carpet for all time to come. For example, it is not inconceivable that China may well recognise India's position on Arunachal Pradesh in exchange for accommodation in Aksai Chin. Whether that would be acceptable to India is, of course, another matter.

With India-China relations progressing steadily and driven increasingly by economics, Pakistan too no longer figures as menacingly as earlier in the development of relations between India and China. China's "all-weather friendship" with Pakistan no longer militates against its growing economic, political and cultural ties with India. Moreover, there have been some nuanced changes in China's attitude to a number of issues between India and Pakistan, as became evident during the 1999 Kargil crisis. The transfer by China of nuclear and missile technology to Pakistan, while worrisome in itself, is not an overriding issue, especially now that India and China have entered into a bilateral security dialogue themselves. One of the underpinnings of this dialogue is the common threat that both countries face from Islamic fundamentalism—India in Kashmir, and China in Xinjiang Province.

On the question of India's permanent membership of the UN Security Council, China is deliberately vague and ambivalent. While it is mindful of India's aspirations, and has said so in as many words, it hides behind the facade of never allowing Japan to become a permanent member of the UN Security Council. Since India's membership was linked together with that of Germany, Japan and Brazil, she has conveniently dodged the issue so far. The US strongly supports the inclusion of both Germany and Japan in any future expansion of the Security Council. Should India's membership, at some future date, be delinked from that of the other three, it would be interesting to see what China's stand would be. In India, this issue arouses strong feelings, because in the 1950s and 60s, when China was consistently denied membership of the UN, it was India that consistently and strongly advocated China's membership to the considerable annoyance of the US, until the US had itself recognised China, and permitted her to occupy the UN seat following the Nixon visit in 1972. As a matter of fact, the US reportedly offered to support India's candidature for a permanent seat in the UN Security Council in the early 1950s, but Nehru, ever the idealist, turned it down saying that it should rightfully go to China (i.e., Communist China replacing the permanent seat then occupied by Taiwan) The same China, whose cause India so robustly espoused—even after the devastating 1962 War—and took cudgels fearlessly on her behalf with the US—today denies India that same opportunity which is rightfully hers by virtue of her size, economy and world stature. Many Indians see this more than simple ingratitude; they see it as a betrayal. More cynical practitioners of international affairs see it simply as China's refusal to cede any strategic space to India—in Asia or out, and particularly in the UN Security Council, where it wants to enjoy its glory in solitude as the sole, undisputed and pre-eminent Asian power.

Also seen as utter betrayal by many Indians is the clandestine support given by China to the rebel insurgencies in India's north-east,[18] to China having acquired a naval presence, if not a proper base, in the Bay of Bengal, thanks to her unfailing support of the ruthless military junta that governs Myanmar and to the deliberate political support (of the "don't worry, we're here" or *"Main hoon na"* variety) extended to all of India's immediate neighbours. Geopoliticians would call this systematic "strategic encirclement" of India by China. After all, how would China feel if India did the same to North Korea, Mongolia, Taiwan and Japan? There is a widespread feeling in India's foreign policy establishment that the aggressive stance of some of India's closest neighbours—not just Pakistan—is entirely due to the political and diplomatic (and often military) support that China liberally extends to these nations, clearly at India's expense.

There is at least one recent example where India was forced to act contrary to the dictates of her national conscience, simply to counter China's overweening influence. This was in Myanmar where India abhorred the military junta and for many years supported the democratic forces in that country led by Aung San Suu Kyi.[19] Then it suddenly woke up in the mid-1990s to find that it had lost all leverage in that country to the Chinese, to the point that it could not even enlist a modicum of assistance from the military junta to prevent rebel insurgents from India's north-east from seeking sanctuary in the rugged hills in the north of the country. Burma (the former name of Myanmar) had historically always been close to India, as it always looked west for political, material and cultural sustenance. Until 1947, like India, it was part of the British Empire and Aung San[20] (the country's first post-Independence leader) enjoyed close relations with Pandit Nehru. Indeed, the remains of India's last Moghul Emperor lie buried in that country. The lower echelons of civil administration of the country before Independence came from India—brought by the British,

18. Contrast this with India's refusal to permit the Dalai Lama to carry out on any anti-China activities from Indian soil, to wit the recent protests by Tibetans against the Olympic torch when it passed through India.

19. The author, who was a Fellow at Harvard University's Center for International Affairs in 1990-91, was told by Suu Kyi's husband, the late Dr.Michael Aris, of his wife's deep sense of hurt at India's *volte face* in Burma.

20. Father of Aung San Suu Kyi, the democratically elected leader of the NLD who has been under house arrest by the ruling military junta of Myanmar since 1990 when she won the national elections.

of course—as were many small merchant businesses that were run by Indians. Yet despite these historical affiliations and geographical proximity, Burma had slipped away from India's diplomatic grasp simply because she joined the western chorus (and her own conscience) of condemnation of the military junta that usurped power in 1990. China was glad to step into the resultant vacuum and the beleaguered, if ruthless, military junta was glad to have a major power on their side, only too willing to fulfill its economic and commercial needs. It was then that India decided to make amends in her overriding national interest—to take care of the insurgency in the northeast but, more important, to offset the almost-exclusive and all-pervasive Chinese influence in that country—not because it suddenly discovered any hitherto-hidden virtues in the military junta that keeps denying the fruits of democracy to its citizens or to free the democratically elected Aung San Suu Kyi from prolonged detention. The Indian Embassy was revamped in 1997 with the dispatch of a top diplomat, Shyam Saran (later India's Foreign Secretary and now Special Envoy of the Prime Minister on the Indo-US Civilian Nuclear Cooperation) and a Presidential Visit to Myanmar took place in 2006.

The only exception in India's neighbourhood where China did not succeed in overriding India's influence is the Himalayan Kingdom of Bhutan. Socio-culturally, as well as ethno-linguistically, akin to the Tibetans, they are perhaps too scared after seeing the fate that has befallen their cousins across the border, to give any quarter to the Chinese. After all it was Mao Zedong himself who had once termed Tibet as the palm of China's hand whose five fingers were Ladakh, Sikkim, Nepal, Bhutan and NEFA (today's Arunachal Pradesh province of India).[21] Of these, a huge part of Ladakh—the Aksai Chin Plateau, is already under China's *de facto* control after they built the Highway (G219) connecting Tibet with Sinkiang; Sikkim opted for merger with India in 1975, Arunachal is claimed, in toto, by the Chinese; and a Maoist regime has just been installed in Nepal (May 2008). Thus, the fear and apprehensions of the Bhutanese become self-evident.

According to the latest Annual Report of India's Defence Ministry (2006-07), "China's military modernisation, with sustained double-digit

---

21. *History of Sino-Indian Relations: Hostile Co-Existence* by John Rowland (1966).

growth in its defence budget for over a decade and continued upgradation of its nuclear and missile assets, development of infrastructure in the India-China border areas and its growing defence links with some of India's neighbors" are a matter of concern to India. It goes on to say that "Chinese assistance to Pakistan's nuclear and missile program has been a matter of concern as it has adversely impacted on India's national security environment. We have also taken note of the recent destruction by China of one of its own satellites in polar orbit through direct ascent anti-satellite test". Interestingly, it also observes that "peace and tranquility continued along the long India-China border as did differences in perception with regard to the boundary issue".

Hu Jintao's visit in November 2006 was the first visit by a Chinese President to India in ten years. The Joint Declaration issued during the visit contained a 10-point roadmap for the development of a "strategic and cooperative partnership" between the two countries. Earlier, Premier Wen Jiabao's visit to India in April 2005 had yielded an important agreement on the political parameters and guiding principles for the settlement of the boundary question.

India and China held their first joint anti-terror military exercise ("Hand-in-Hand, 2007") in Kunming, Yunnan, in December 2007. While there was considerable hype in the media about how far military ties between the giant neighbours had come since the eyeball confrontation of 1962, the fact is that China has held similar exercises with the armed forces of different countries on at least eight occasions since 2002 and involved no more than about 100 troops from each side. The official mouthpiece, *People's Daily* (26 December 2007) said: "Although some military and diplomatic observers said that the joint training is more symbolic than substantial, many acknowledged that the point is not the scale of the joint training or what specific anti-terrorism skills are involved. The point is that the soldiers on both sides are moving toward each other in a friendly way." If this is what the 'strategic cooperative partnership' between the two countries, is all about, clearly a great deal more needs to be done.

Prime Minister Manmohan Singh visited China in January 2008 during which "A Shared Vision for the 21st Century" was signed. A spokesman of the Chinese Foreign Ministry stated after the Prime Minister's meeting with President Hu Jintao that the visit would have "long-term and significant" impact on the bilateral relations between India and China, describing the joint document as a "milestone," he said that it was "a signal of the big step forward in the history of bilateral relations." He further added that it was "a message to the outside world that the two sides will intensify their cooperation to build a harmonious world." The visit and talks, according to him were a "reflection of the political will" of both sides to "press ahead" with their bilateral ties. Asked specifically whether China would support India's quest for permanent membership of the UN Security Council, he said "India is a major developing country. China understands and supports the aspirations of India to play a larger role in international organisations, including UN". In other words, beyond a statement of good intentions, China is not ready to commit any support to India's legitimate quest for a seat on the UN Security Council as a permanent member.

Besides keeping the dialogue going at the highest level, which arguably is an achievement in itself, nothing concrete emerged from the visit in terms of, for example the boundary question. After nearly a dozen meetings of the Joint Working Group, even "peace and tranquillity" on the border is somewhat suspect if the numerous reports in the media are to be believed about PLA patrols deep inside the 'finger'area of Sikkim, and elsewhere along the border.

It is against this backdrop that we have to consider the way ahead in India-China relations. The negative vibes come mainly from recent history—the past five decades which have seen more downsides than upsides, as a result of which lingering doubts and nagging suspicions will continue to haunt the relationship, until at least the present generation passes away from the scene. The positive indications come from the current management of the relationship—a pragmatic approach by both sides to press ahead with the future. The biggest challenge for both India and China is to overcome the trust deficit that pervasively lingers in their mutual dealings and take bold steps well beyond the "candy floss of bloated sugar-coated verbiage which makes little difference to realpolitik" as a seasoned commentator on Sino-Indian relations put it.

3 | The US-China Relationship

SECTION I

THE PAST

We should not look at China through rose colored glasses, nor should we look through a glass darkly to see an image that distorts China's strength and ignores its complexities. We need to see China clearly, its progress and its problems, its system and its strains, its policies and its perceptions of us, of itself, of the world.

President Clinton
April 1999

The US-China relationship has, since the advent of the communist government on the Chinese mainland in 1949, gone through phases ranging from eyeball-to-eyeball confrontation (late 40s) to bitter hostility (50s), to calculated understanding (60s), to warmth (70s), to friendship (80s), to suspicion (90s) and finally to confusion from being unable to figure out whether it is actually a 'strategic partner' or a 'strategic competitor'.

The civil war in China between the communists led by Mao Zedong and the nationalists led by Chiang Kai-shek partly overlapped with the Second World War, but then continued beyond the waning years of the War as each side tried to establish its supremacy on the mainland. In this struggle, which lasted a good four years, the US was strongly supporting the Nationalists (or KMT—Kuo Min Tang) against the Communists (or CCP—Chinese Communist Party) for the simple reason that the latter were on the other side of the ideological divide. Equally naturally, the Chinese communists were receiving generous quantities of aid and even more generous political support from the Soviet Union. Welcome to the front row seats of the first show of the Cold War, a war which played without a break for the ensuing half a century.

It would perhaps be correct to say that the Chinese civil war became part of the larger theatre of WWII because while the Nationalists and Communists bitterly fought each other, they were also fighting against the Japanese who had been steadily making inroads into China ever since the early 20th century.[1] Indeed both sides—the KMT and CCP—accused each other of fighting more robustly among themselves than fighting the Japanese, who were obviously a greater danger.[2] Once the WWII ended with US intervention in 1945, one of the bones of contentions between these two bitter rivals was as to who gets to keep the (Japanese) spoils left behind in China after Japan's surrender, given the large (military) presence and (commercial) interests they had built up over the years in many parts of China, and particularly in Manchuria. As a matter of fact, in many instances the US actually directed the Japanese to surrender to the Nationalists (KMT) even when the Communists (CCP) got there first.

While the Nationalist Chinese forces claimed political legitimacy and the reigns of national government during the interregnum between end of WWII and the end of the civil war in China, the Communist forces under Mao Zedong held significant political leverage, especially in the rural areas where capitalist reforms had often yielded harsh and intolerable working conditions for the peasantry. The US, as stated above, was clearly and openly supportive of the Nationalists and did everything possible in the closing years of the Chinese civil war to help them gain power in Peking. Chiang Kai-shek, of course, kept complaining that it was a case of too little, too late, as the communists kept gaining one victory after another over the nationalist forces. Apart from pervasive corruption throughout the ranks and low morale, the other reason for the rout of the KMT was the strong perception in the minds of the people that they were never serious about fighting the Japanese—an exploitative foreign power on Chinese soil whom the people saw as the greater enemy. Add to this the fact that with their bases in the rural areas, the communists had built a very large swathe of support among the peasants and other poor masses, amongst whom they lived and toiled, whereas the Nationalists were comfortably ensconced in

---

1.	The Japanese invaded and occupied Manchuria in 1931.

2.	Nationalist (KMT) leader, Chiang Kai-shek famously said that the Japanese were a 'disease of the skin' whereas the (Chinese) communists were a 'disease of the bone', implying that the fight against the latter was more important.

the cities, unmindful of the hardships of the common folk. Eventually, it was this support of the people at the grassroots level that helped the CCP gain victory after victory over the KMT forces and eventually the reigns of state power in Peking.

Even after the fall of the KMT and the establishment of the Nationalist government on the island of Formosa (Taiwan), the US persisted in its anti-Communist policy, recognising the Chiang Kai-shek-led government as the sole legitimate authority over (the whole of) China. As a result, the Nationalist KMT government based in Taiwan continued to hold China's seat in the United Nations, including the permanent membership of the UN Security Council, calling itself the Republic of China (ROC). In response, the Chinese Communist government (now called the PRC— People's Republic of China to distinguish itself from the regime in Taiwan) regarded the US as the biggest enemy of the Chinese people. No formal relations were to be established between these two nations until Nixon's path breaking 1972 visit to China, decades after the Communist takeover. The bulk of the nation's propaganda machinery during this time (and even after 1972 till formal diplomatic relations were established in 1979) was geared to attacking American "imperialism", "capitalism", "hegemonism" and worse. Until then, as far as the Chinese communist regime was concerned, America epitomised everything that was evil, exploitative, sinful, malevolent, wicked and downright immoral. The indoctrination started very early in childhood. Toy guns sold in China, for example, invariably had the stars and stripes for target practice and every negative caricature was drawn with an American theme. No reference to the US could be made in the media or public pronouncements without prefixing or suffixing it with an epithet like "imperialism" or "imperialists", usually accompanied by a more derogatory term or two like "running dog".[3]

Tensions between the US and China erupted on several occasions. The first of these arose soon after the communists had assumed the reins of power in Peking and took the ugly form of an eyeball-to-eyeball confrontation with the Chinese PLA (Peoples' Liberation Army) in Korea.

---

3. The author, who lived in Beijing during the historic Nixon visit recalls asking a junior Chinese official how President Nixon could be invited to China if he and his country were the epitome of all that was evil? The swift reply was "We did not invite Nixon. He invited himself" and went on to graphically illustrate how even in the past ages many undesirable vassals had come to pay obeisance to the Emperor—the son of Heaven—in Beijing.

The war in Korea was being fought between the North Korean invading forces and US-led UN defenders, when China decided to send what it called "Chinese Peoples Volunteers" to help North Korea. Prior to China's intervention, the UN forces had succeeded in not just driving North Korean forces from South Korea, but had advanced as far as the Yalu River separating China and North Korea. Chinese entrance into the war reversed much of that success, as wave after human wave of Chinese PLA soldiers (calling themselves 'volunteers') pushed the US-led UN troops well South, almost near Seoul, until an armistice was signed in 1953, splitting the peninsula along a demilitarised zone (DMZ) at the 38th North parallel.

Taiwan's Straits crises of 1954-55 and 1958, when China shelled the Taiwanese islands of Quemoy and Matsu in a bid to force the integration of Taiwan with the mainland, brought US intervention in the Straits, and even the deployment of nuclear weapons was considered.

Economic sanctions invoked by the US against China succeeded in driving Moscow and Beijing closer than ever, a bond only increased in strength by the US' active policy of containment of the Communist nation during the 50s and 60s. This Sino-Soviet friendship lasted until a rift developed between Moscow and Beijing by the mid 1960s. Initially this rift was seemingly ideological, with China accusing the Soviet leadership of "revisionism"—a euphemism for desertion or abandonment of hard-core Marxist-Leninist dogma. Later, with passage of time, it became increasingly clear that behind this veil of accusations about "revisionism" lay more mundane issues of national interest like cooperation in the economic and military spheres and sharing of nuclear weapons technology. Beyond a point, the Soviets became parsimonious about both. They withheld critical technology and components when it came to China's quest for nuclear power—either fearing potential rivalry or simply not wanting another communist nuclear power to upset the USSR's monopoly. In the economic sphere, they were similarly loathe to part with their latest technologies, passing on, instead, outmoded technologies no longer of any use to them. When China complained, the Soviets just simply withdrew all assistance and walked away, convinced that such a move would surely rub Chinese noses to the ground. Indeed all Soviet engineers and technicians in China returned home in 1960. But then politics is known to make strange bedfellows, as the Soviets realised to their peril a few years later.

A third occasion of heightened tensions was the Sino-Indian War of 1962. As far as the US was concerned, it was yet another example of a Communist nation invading a democratic state, and also was seen as an opportunity to gain a new ally. While critical of India for its non-aligned foreign policy, the US dispensed small amounts of aid to India—whose psychological impact far outweighed its military utility! However, it must in all fairness be pointed out, that it was a time when President John F Kennedy was preoccupied with the Cuban Missile Crisis at America's very doorstep, and thus the aid arrived in too small a quantity to make any significant impact and too late to alter the outcome of the war. Further, in 1963 Kennedy met with his advisors to discuss the possibility of the use of nuclear weapons against China if another invasion of India were to occur.[4]

However, despite such differences and conflicts, the US did not blind itself to the reality that a nation of China's size, population, and economic capacity would soon become a major player in world affairs.[5] The US understood that one day it would have to deal with China. The opportunity to do so presented itself not long after the Sino-Indian war. The Soviet Union, once a great ally of China after the signing of the 1950 "Sino-Soviet Treaty of Friendship, Alliance, and Mutual Assistance", had rapidly fallen out of favour, and by 1963 was the subject of ideological barbs from Mao. The US took advantage of this situation, and sought to commence a diplomatic dialogue with China. However, such parleys were 'unofficial' and conducted in great secrecy, generally taking place in safe third-country locations such as Geneva or in countries like Rumania, Poland, and Pakistan. Kissinger used Pakistan as the conduit through which he was able to arrange the first breakthrough in modern Sino-US relations, flying secretly from an air force base in Peshawar to Peking in 1971 for the initial high-level contacts that eventually resulted in the historic Nixon visit to China in 1972. Earlier 'direct' contacts were through "Ping Pong Diplomacy", so-called because of the exchange of US and Chinese national ping pong players was the first act of 'breaking-the-ice' between these nations.

---

4. Declassified record in the John F. Kennedy Presidential Library and Museum in Boston of the US National Security Council Meeting, May 9, 1963.

5. Between 1954 and 1970, US and PRC met 136 times through their Ambassadors in Geneva and Warsaw.

The Nixon visit was monumental in its significance. The myth of the 'communist monolith' lay shattered. American diplomacy had succeeded in exploiting the wedge between the two communist giants to isolate the Soviet Union, and draw China to its side. The discourse at this meeting helped set the tone of interactions between China and the US that has lasted for decades. The most important of the issues discussed were those regarding Taiwan, still a close American ally. Bilateral discussions during the visit culminated in the issuance of the Shanghai Communiqué. The Communiqué stated that both sides believed there was only one China and Taiwan was part of that China. This stance has allowed for the creation of a status quo, howsoever uneasy, that has held to this day.

The relationship between the two nations continued to make important strides. In 1975 Gerald Ford became the second US President to visit China. Formal diplomatic recognition followed in 1979 and a visit by Deng Xiaoping to the US in the same year. While the US did pass the Taiwan Relations Act reaffirming strong ties with the island in that same year, the relationship with China was not put under undue stress as a result (though China did express public disapproval). However, many of the diplomatic obstacles faced by China and the US over the next decade revolved around the twin issues of the Island's security (from forcible incorporation by the government on the Mainland) and arms sales to Taiwan, a stance that has been reaffirmed by successive US Presidents. By 1980, however, the US did agree that while it would not stop arms sales to Taiwan, it would not increase them and would consider reducing them over time.

A major roadblock in US-China relations was encountered in June 1989 as a result of the Tiananmen Square Massacre. Taking place just months after George HW Bush's visit, the US and many nations of the world over responded with significant trade sanctions and an arms embargo against China. From then on much of the US policy towards China has hinged upon China's human rights record. In 1993 President Bill Clinton stated that China's 'Most Favoured Nation' status in international trade should be based upon its human rights record. Taiwan continued to be a major issue of interest to both nations, and from 1995-96 a visit by Taiwanese President Lee Tenghui to speak at Cornell University set off a chain of vociferous protests by China, from the withdrawal of its ambassador in 1995 to war games off the coast of Taiwan in 1996.

The Third Taiwan Strait Crisis in 1996 originated from the missile tests conducted by China in the waters surrounding Taiwan to send a strong signal to the Island's government under President Lee Teng-hui, who was perceived as moving Taiwan towards Independence and thus away from the One-China policy. It was also intended to intimidate the Taiwanese electorate in the run-up to the 1996 presidential election. In each case fear of US intervention ensured that the crisis did not get out of hand.

In the early 21st century relations between the US and China have remained tense at best. President Bush visited China in 2002 to celebrate the 30th anniversary of Nixon's visit, and the US government released statements that accused China of modernising its military to prepare for an invasion of Taiwan. While China has responded that their programme is purely for national defence, its Anti-Secession Law of 2005, stating that China will use non-peaceful means to deal with Taiwan if it officially declares independence, has done little to allay those misgivings and suspicions. In 2007, China made its "modernisation" efforts obvious by destroying an aging spy satellite using highly-sophisticated missile technology. While made to look like a routine exercise, it became abundantly clear, China was signaling that militarily and technologically, it was no longer far behind other major powers. However, not all trends indicate a divergence between Beijing and Washington, as shown by the joint effort by China and the US to diffuse the North Korean nuclear threat and participate in the 6-nation initiative to curb, if not end, that country's dangerous nuclear ambitions.

The accidental bombing of China's Belgrade embassy by NATO warplanes in 1999, and a collision between a US spy plane and a Chinese fighter jet in the South China Sea in 2001 impacted negatively on the bilateral relations in recent years. The US Congress awarding its highest civilian honour to the Dalai Lama in 2007 and renewed arms sales to Taiwan, including an Anti-Missile Defense System the same year led China to retaliate by a last-minute notice to bar the aircraft carrier USS

Kitty Hawk and its escort vessels from entering Hong Kong harbour for a routine refueling and resupplying visit during Thanksgiving (2007).

Of significant interest are also the economic affairs between China and the US. At present China has allowed no nation but Taiwan to accrue a trade deficit against it and the US is no exception. The US trade deficit towards China has grown exponentially, from $33 billion in 1992 to reach an all-time high of $256 billion in 2007. Many feel that this gross imbalance is the result of unfair trade practices, including currency manipulation, and has contributed to the loss of 3 million US manufacturing jobs since 2001. Conflict between the two nations has grown over the Chinese Yuan, which has been pegged to the dollar—unfairly, charges the US, to keep the price of its exports artificially low. In doing this, China guarantees that its goods will be cheap for the US to import, but not vice versa. Further, China has invested significantly in the dollar. It is estimated to hold nearly $1 trillion in US dollar assets. In comparison, the total number of dollars in circulation is $1.3 trillion. If China were to start dumping its dollars, US interest rates would spike, inflation would soar, the housing market would get pummeled, and the economy would likely plunge into a serious recession. To keep its currency relative to the dollar, China takes its trade profits and buys US treasuries, effectively investing the trade profits back in the US. This has greatly benefited America by providing easy debt to finance its expenditures.

By keeping its currency undervalued, China not only keeps its factories running and thus provide employment to millions of her citizens, but it also supplies America with dangerously easy debt. Like a drug dealer supplying cocaine, China provides easy loans to US financial institutions who have thus become addicted to the artificial short-term benefits supplied by Chinese lending.

The US has lately been holding regular consultations with China under the mechanism of the 'Strategic Dialogue' on political matters and the 'Strategic Economic Dialogue' on economic matters, including trade, fiscal and monetary issues.

Bi-annual meetings of the 'Strategic Economic Dialogue' were mooted in 2006, to be held alternately in China and the US. The most recent of these—the fourth since its establishment—was held in Annapolis, Maryland in June 2008 but clearly achieved little by way of cooling down the simmering trade tensions revolving around issues like revaluation of the Yuan and correcting the highly-skewed trade imbalance. Also discussed were the measures to boost energy security, lowering global pollution and expanding food monitoring. The American side apparently expressed their unhappiness over the slow pace of China's economic reforms telling their guests about the number of bills introduced in Congress that would impose economic sanctions on China unless the country moves more quickly to allow its currency to rise in value against the dollar. In keeping with classic Chinese negotiating tactics, Zhou Xiachuan, the head of China's central bank and a member of the Chinese delegation at the talks said that the weak dollar was not a specific topic of discussion.[6] Turning the tables, he asked instead to be briefed about the regulatory mistakes that had been made that contributed to the subprime mortgage crisis.

While China has allowed its currency to rise in value by 20 per cent against the dollar since July 2005, the US feels that this correction is grossly inadequate and more needs to be done (US estimates it at 45 per cent) and still puts US products at a competitive disadvantage.

Other points of contention on the economic front are the US desire to see the Chinese open up its financial sector to foreign banks and investment houses to which China is strongly opposed; measures for stricter safety inspection of food products and toys exported to the US, and protection of IPRs. Millions of US patented wares—from computer software to film and TV shows, to music—are openly sold in China, and also exported to various destinations in Asia, Africa and the Middle East where copyright legislation is either absent or weak. These are exported by Chinese businessmen with the PRC government simply turning a blind eye, except for the occasional public destruction of such pirated materials.

Then, there are also allegations that China stole US nuclear secrets from the Los Alamos National Laboratory, and that US satellite companies transferred sensitive missile technology to China in the late 90s and early 2000s.

---

6. Chinese officials have been saying openly that the dollar's decline against other currencies has contributed to rising global prices for oil, food and other commodities.

SECTION II

CHALLENGES AND OPPORTUNITIES

Whatever changes take place in the United States and the international situation, our guideline of developing constructive, cooperative relations with the United States remains unchanged........Furthering the Sino-U.S. relationship conforms to the fundamental interest of the two countries and peoples, and influences peace, stability and development regionally and worldwide.

President Hu Jintao
Beijing, 30 June 2008

Despite faltering beginnings, a disastrous economic experiment with the infamous "Great Leap Forward" in the 50s and an equally disastrous political experiment by way of the "Great Proletarian Cultural Revolution" in the late 60s and early 70s, China has made tremendous strides since its emergence on to the world stage in 1949. No longer a country known for its unstable government and backward economy, China is now a political and military heavyweight in world affairs, and when it comes to economics, undoubtedly a manufacturing and exporting superpower. The fact that the country played host to the Summer Olympics in 2008, having outmaneuvered the likes of Paris and Toronto is a testament to the country's global clout today.[7]

That China is on the rise today is beyond dispute. The question that everyone in the world is asking is what kind of shape that "rise" is likely to assume? Like the proverbial blind men and the elephant, China's rise means different things to different countries. It is not easy to forget that the country still upholds a system that is embraced by fewer and fewer nations, and has been abandoned by most of its most fervent adherents. That system pays scant regard to human rights and related values that modern democratic societies hold dear. That is why the US and the West distanced themselves from China after the Tiananmen incidents of 1989 with some of the sanctions (e.g., on export of Arms) still in place until today. It is a system that can demand of its citizens that each couple only have one child. Every now and then one hears about death row prisoners in Chinese jails having their organs "voluntarily" removed for

---

7.   Steven Spielberg dropped out in February 2008 as an artistic adviser to the Olympic Games in protest against Chinese policies in Darfur. In March 2008, rioting in Tibet was followed by pro-Tibet protests on the torch relay at several world capitals including London and Paris, besides San Francisco, Athens etc.

transplantation. Executions and disappearances of dissidents are not uncommon. The Falun Gong, an alternative way to improve spiritual and physical health much like Yoga, is banned in China and its websites blocked by the communist Government.[8]

The secrecy that surrounds China's military build-up is another matter of deep concern, not only to the US, but also to countries in the immediate neighbourhood like Japan, India, South Korea, Taiwan, Vietnam etc. In the past decade, China has made the modernisation and build-up of its military a matter of top national priority. While it claims to have only 17.8 per cent of its economy dedicated to the military, the US projects that the true figure might be anywhere up three times larger. This is of significant interest to the US due to China's continued conflict with Taiwan. The Anti-Secession Act of 2005 has made diplomatic resolution of the Taiwan issue far more difficult. Any attempt by China to use force to solve the Taiwan issue would inevitably invite US involvement, and thus any Chinese military buildup is of grave concern to the US. This places a strain upon already testy relations between China, the US, and Taiwan.

Politically, China finds itself far less isolated than it was in the middle of the 20th century. It has worked hard to cultivate relations with its Asian neighbours, as well as increase its influence with Africa with generous "donations" and other forms of backing to these nations. It is clear China covets Africa for its large untapped natural resources, as well as its mostly uninfluenced political entities. While for the most part all such assistance is of great help to the African countries, there are negative fallouts too, as is the case with the ongoing genocide in Darfur. Apart from not exerting its influence upon the Government of Sudan to end the atrocities in Darfur spearheaded by the government-supported Janjawid militias, China is also the main supplier of arms to the government with which it carries out these atrocities. The same is true of Zimbabwe where the ruinous depredations of Robert Mugabe are greatly facilitated by the uninterrupted supply of Chinese arms and munitions with which his forces suppress any opposition. China may take the stance that these are purely commercial

---

8. Fa "means the law and principles of the universe, "Lun" means wheel, "Gong" is an abbreviation of "Qigong" which means "cultivation and practice." Falun Gong is thus the "cultivation and practice of the great law wheel." Its practice comprises essentially a moral philosophy for self-improvement, and 5 sets of exercises involving lotus postures and hand movements with the help of Chinese music.

transactions between sovereign governments, but China's growing stature in the world demands a certain social and moral responsibility. It is areas such as these which present both a challenge in US-China relations as well as an opportunity, because the only country which has, or conceivably could have, that kind of influence over China would be the US.

Given the political will, China can do it. After all, Hong Kong was peacefully reintegrated with the mainland through the imaginative "One Nation, Two Systems" plan. It was supposed to be a model for Taiwan, except that Taiwan's history and geography is very different to that of Hong Kong, and in any case no one in Taiwan has shown any inclination to accept that formula. At least that was the stand till recently. With a KMT-led government recently installed in Taipei that is more sensitive to the concerns of the Mainland, there may well be a serious reconsideration of the options available other than an indefinite extension of the status quo.

China's consonance with the US in the domains of suppression of terrorism and prevention of nuclear proliferation has helped the two nations to politically re-sculpt their respective landscapes. No longer is either one a sole ideological foe, as they have found something in common to direct their energies against. However, a major issue that arises as to each nation's respective definitions of terrorism. China condemns the independence movements in Xinjiang and Tibet as terrorist or secessionist in nature. The Chinese have repeatedly tried to paint their own campaign against Uighur separatists in Xinjiang and the Dalai Lama's supporters in Tibet as a flank of the US-led war on terrorism to get America to drop its long-standing protests over Chinese human rights abuses in its crackdowns in Xinjiang and Tibet.

The Dalai Lama, however, enjoys great support among the American people and is held in great esteem by its leadership as the political and religious leader in-exile of Tibet, who won the Nobel Peace Prize in 1989. As expected, China responded to this award with "utmost regret and indignation", adding quite incredulously that the decision of the Nobel Committee "deviates from the committee's purpose of awarding the prize to those working for and contributing to harmony and good will among peoples". Quite on the contrary, it is precisely because he is tirelessly "working for and contributing to harmony and good will among peoples" that he has been and continues to be graciously and warmly received by freedom-loving people and their leaders all over the world. President Bush has received the 72-year old Tibetan spiritual leader in the White House three times in six years. It was the third meeting in six years between the president and on 17 October 2007 he also attended the ceremony at the US Capitol where the Dalai Lama received the Congressional Gold Medal, the top US civilian award. Out of deference to China's sensitivities, President Bush met the Dalai Lama in the White House rather than the Oval Office. In September 2007, His Holiness was similarly received by the German Chancellor Angela Merkel. Around the same time he was also received by Austrian Chancellor Alfred Gusenbauer, Australian Prime Minister John Howard and Canadian Prime Minister Stephen Harper. All such meetings invite Chinese wrath and denunciation even though all the Dalai Lama does is to explain the rationale for his demand for human rights in Tibet and genuine autonomy, not independence, to enable Tibetans to freely practice their religion and traditional culture. After all this is what China promised the Tibetan people when it was annexed against their will in 1951. China must be persuaded to improve her human rights record rather than routinely condemn the Dalai Lama whom all Tibetans revere as their God-King. China's answer to this is to counter US condemnation by creating a yearly White Paper since 1998 in which it records human rights violations allegedly committed by the US during that year, and also serves as proof of Chinese progress in that domain. In 2007, China's White Paper specifically focused on its progress towards democracy, outlining the activities and role of the Communist and non-Communist Parties in China.

There is plenty to do on the economic front too. The US suffers a massive trade deficit with China. In 2006, while US exports to China increased 20 per cent from 2004, imports over the same period increased from $104 billion to $243.5 billion, showing a disproportionate increase in an already significant trade deficit. This can be attributed to limitations imposed by China as to US access to Chinese markets, the artificial value of the Yuan, and, according to the State Department, due to the increased demand by other East Asian nations to use China as a final assembly point for products intended for export, and thus a transfer of export from that nation to China. Overall, however, the US has a GDP six times larger than China while China has four times the population. While China's ascent to the World Trade Organisation in 2001 was meant to correct these issues, more work is left to be done before a true trade balance is struck.

While China accelerates her economic development in order to keep pace with the growth of her economy, she faces some major disadvantages. The growing demand for jobs within China places a greater stress on her economy to provide them. The rapid growth is leading to environmental deterioration and is increasingly becoming a critical issue. Energy consumption and demand, as well as pollution and water scarcity will increase exponentially in China in the foreseeable future. These issues are at present only beginning to be realised, but will undoubtedly become central to the future relationship between China and the US.

The challenge before the US, as far as China is concerned, is to nudge her in seeing the benefits of greater degree of transparency in her dealings internally with her own citizenry and externally with the rest of the world so that China's unstoppable rise is not always accompanied by the big question mark, "But will it be peaceful?" The reason for this obviously lies in the dismal record of China's past—starting with her military adventurism in Korea (1951) so soon after the declaration of the new "People's Republic" (1949), to her determined push to "export" communism in Southeast Asia in the 1950s and 60s, the attack on India across the Himalayas (1962), the attack on Russia in the Ussuri River Sector (1969), excesses committed against foreign countries and their Embassies during the GPCR (1966-1976), and after the economic reforms that began with the 'four modernisations', to an aggressive flooding of cheap Chinese consumer goods throughout markets in Southeast Asia, often at the cost of small-scale industries in these countries. China's repeated shelling of the Taiwanese islands of Quemoy and Matsu, the "teaching a lesson" to Vietnam in 1988 and her claims over the Paracel and Spratly Islands[9] in the South China Sea (with forcible occupation of the Paracel Islands in 1976) has done little in the way of inspiring confidence in China's "peaceful rise" among her neighbours. Internally,

---

9. China claims both the Paracel and Spratly Islands in the South China Sea, which it calls 'Xisha' and 'Nansha' respectively. In 1976, China enforced its claim upon the Paracel Islands by seizing them from Vietnam.

the incredible loss of life[10] resulting from failure of the experiments with rural communes in the 1950s, the disastrous 'Great Leap Forward' and the 'Great Proletarian Cultural Revolution' and Tiananmen 1989, not to mention the repression of Tibetans and Uighurs (in Sinkiang) has led to serious questions about China's Human Rights record. Repeated assertions in international forums by China that these are 'internal matters' that brook no external interference may pass muster for official records, but cut no ice with an apprehensive international community that is appalled by China's continued support to rogue regimes in countries like Sudan, Myanmar and Zimbabwe—rife with internal repression, bordering on genocide at least in one case. There is an increasing feeling in the international community that but for China's patronage—material as well as diplomatic (in the UN)—these regimes would fall. Of course there are limits to US's ability to bring about such a change, especially at a time when her economic relationship with China is so incredibly skewed in the latter's favour. In spite of that, or perhaps because of it, the US alone that has enough leverage, and capacity for global leadership, if only adequately supplemented by the requisite political will, to nudge China into shouldering international responsibilities in a manner that does not arouse fears of many in the world community. As Secretary of State Condoleezza Rice rightly said in the July/August 2008 issue of *Foreign Affairs*:

> The last eight years have challenged us to deal with rising Chinese influence, something we have no reason to fear *if that power is used responsibly*. We have stressed to Beijing that with China's full membership in the international community comes responsibilities, whether in the conduct of economic and trade policy, its approach to energy and the environment, or its policies in the developing world. (Emphasis mine).

Elsewhere in the same article, the US Secretary of State also spoke about China's lack of transparency about its military spending, military doctrine and strategic goals that only leads to increased mistrust and suspicion, but added that the US sustains an active and candid dialogue with China's leaders on these challenges. Clearly it needs to be emphasised that China carries a special responsibility as a permanent member of the UN Security Council when it comes to such vital issues. The US believes that in some areas it has, indeed, been able to secure China's understanding, as for example in the six-party talks on the North Korean nuclear issue. While that is still some ways away from a satisfactory

---

10. Unconfirmed but reliable estimates of killed run into millions,

resolution, the US feels that it could not have achieved, whatever little has been achieved so far, without China's active cooperation.

SECTION III

THE WAY AHEAD

It is idiotic to contemplate a future that is anything other than one of cooperation between China and the US for future prosperity. But on the other hand, it will be foolish not to prepare for the worst.

Bill Clinton

This quotation by a politically-astute US President fairly neatly sums up the future of the US-China relationship. It took nearly a quarter of a century for the US to come to terms with their state of denial about which was the "real" China—the one on the Mainland or the one on the Island of Taiwan? Most of the rest of the world, except for US and its hard core allies, had long since seen the writing on the wall. In the US, it required a Kissinger to wake Nixon up and get his and America's national mindset to come to grip with ground realities. The timing was spurred on by the cracks appearing in the communist camp; it was now left for American diplomacy to drive the wedge hard and wide enough to tear apart the fabric of international communism. All that was set in motion with the historic visit of President Nixon to China in 1972.

A little less than two decades later the other communist giant abandoned communism and the Cold War came to a formal end. After the end of the Cold War following the collapse of the Soviet Union, the world is witnessing the emergence of China as a potential threat to US supremacy not only in the Asia-Pacific but possibly beyond. It began with economics and has since spilled over to other areas—notably human rights, politics and military preparedness etc.

As for Taiwan, the reality of this "conflict" today is that unless there is something like a crude attempt by Taiwan to declare Independence and China retaliates to take the island by force, war between the US and China is highly unlikely. Diplomatic spats on the magnitude of those exchanged between the US and the Soviet Union during the Cold War may not be uncommon,[11] but the central theme of maintaining the economic status quo that serves as a dominating influence in both countries will most likely prevent any military conflict. America serves as a crucial outlet to China's global exports, just as much as the US knows a significant share of the welfare of its currency is controlled by China. Because of the influence of both in world economic affairs, any sudden depreciation of currency or an economic downturn in either country due to war would be clearly disastrous. Thus, war is not just unhealthy for China or the US, it is unhealthy for the world at large.

What will more likely take place, however, is a new form of warfare—a war of science. An arms race between the two countries appears inevitable. This race won't be in the form of what was as open and threatening as the Cold War, but rather be a scientific arms race. This war may be in the patent office, the research laboratory, and at international conferences. There is and will continue to be an understanding that a country's military exploits against another are no longer what distinguishes one as a world power, but rather that country's prestige when matched up against other nations. It is quality of life, average lifespan, level of medical, computer, engineering, and physics knowledge, all this is what makes one a superpower. Espionage will no longer be used primarily to obtain a country's military position and planned movements, but rather its technological standing and focus of research programmes. A foretaste of this scientific war was recently provided by China's successful shooting down of an ageing missile in outer space. Thus, even if it a war of science, it could well have military applications.

Diplomatic maneuverings of the past may well give way to technological revolutions, such as India and China are experiencing today, or those that continue to lead the world in global production and economic organisation and trade, such as Japan, the US, and Germany. In Thomas L Friedman's *The World is Flat*, we learn of the advent of technology transfer between the US and India. India is at the point of technological progression that the US had attained during its information revolution of the mid 20th century. As a result, the US invests in this burgeoning yet still cheap economy. No longer do we speak to tech support for many

---

11. Such as during the accidental bombing of the Chinese Embassy in Belgrade, the EP3 plane incident.

common appliances in this country. India now handles this channel of information. Much the same in the manufacturing sector has and will continue to take place in China.[12]

China also presents an interesting situation, where a currency that is held at an artificially cheap margin dominates international economic markets, especially of buyer's economies such as that of the US. The greatest conflict between these two nations will be over the value of Chinese currency. Despite pleas from the US for China to re-evaluate the Yuan, there has and will not be any significant movement in that direction by China. The cheap value of the Yuan makes export of labour and technology from the US to China near lucrative, attracting industry and contracts away from the US. Such ability to control US's investment strategies through complete control of a cheap currency is far more powerful than the shockwave and damage created by any warfare. Just as OPEC had shown the US in the 1970s the power it has over the dollar, China need just say the word to divest its holdings of the dollar and watch the currency come crashing down. The only reason that it will not do so is because she herself is the largest holder of the currency, and any precipitate action would be tantamount to cutting one's nose to spite one's face.

However, despite the advent of technological wars, there are still military considerations. Such considerations stem from provinces and conflicts that are old and longstanding. The most noteworthy of these issues are Tibet and Taiwan.

The situation regarding Tibet, all moral and political issues taken into consideration, must be considered moot. In the style of the US during its 'Manifest Destiny' period, China has moved such a large contingent of settlers into the region that the Tibetan nationals no longer constitute a majority of the population. Even if a plebiscite were to be forced by international pressure, the outcome would legitimately point to China as sovereign over the area, human rights violations take place on a continuing basis. The lives of many religious Buddhists are lost for the sole crime of worshipping as they please. However, regardless of this infraction, there will be no change in the status of Tibet. Today China claims significant progress in Tibet due to its leadership as, for political as

12.   Friedman, 2007. p. 40.

well as economic reasons, a roadway and rail-link infrastructure has been created to modernise the Tibetan state, establishments that had not been seen before in the province's history. Taking all these circumstances into consideration, the Free Tibet movement will have been in vain and the province is now firmly and irrevocably in China's hands. All that countries like the US, EU or India do is to use their powers of persuasion, on their own or through human rights groups, to permit freedom of worship in, and the preservation of the culture, traditions and heritage of the Tibetan people who are ethnically, linguistically and by another yardstick, a people very different from the Han Chinese.

Taiwan provides a more interesting set of circumstances. Taiwan, unlike Tibet, is not just economically advanced as a quasi-independent state, it also has the US bound by treaty agreement to support it in the case of any Chinese attempt to retake the territory by force, all the talk of China's "sacred duty" in "reuniting" the runaway province with the "Motherland" notwithstanding. The US has reaffirmed this treaty on several occasions, and actively makes arms deals with the Taiwanese. The threat of war reached heights at incremental periods over the 20th century, and reached an additional apex in the 21st, when Jiang Zemin openly stated that any movement towards Taiwanese independence would evoke an instant aggressive response. Chinese batteries from the mainland are trained on Taiwan, and hostilities promise to claim millions of lives.

Even in the potentially explosive situation with regard to Taiwan, war is unlikely. Taiwan, in its status as one of the premiere trading powers of Asia, would not just command US but world condemnation and support if the Chinese were to move against what it regards as its own 'renegade' province. The new international language is money, and it is not cost feasible to find a new replacement trading partner if Taiwan were to be annexed by military means, a solution that would without question cripple its economy for years to come through damage and death from invasion. In addition, Taiwan is the only country that has a trade surplus with China, something that would surely damage the Chinese economy if tampered with. A conflict with the potential for a quick escalation between two nuclear powers also threatens the use of these weapons, an instant guarantee of détente and a prevention of the escalation of conflict. In his text *From Chivalry to Terrorism: War and the Changing Nature of Masculinity*, Leo Braudy states that the Soviet Union and the US did not go to war because as mature governments they understood what that war would mean.[13] Similarly, they recognised the importance of not using nuclear arms, a decision not just made in Korea, but again in Vietnam, to prevent Mutually Assured Destruction (MAD).

On the converse, however, China would reclaim its trade debt with Taiwan if the province were to be annexed into its sphere. This might serve as clear reasoning why Taiwan is the only country to have a trade surplus with China, and China has consented to be in this situation. Furthermore, as noted by Robert Ash in *China Quarterly*, there is immense advantage to Hong Kong and Taiwan expanding onto the Chinese mainland, thus giving mainland China further capital and advancement technologically within its own local sphere of influence.[14] Therefore, in this case and only this case, a significant economic advantage would go to China if Taiwan were to be persuaded to "reunify" peacefully. China continually views, and views correctly, that Japan is the primary trading threat to Chinese trade influence in both East Asia and the rest of the globe. Absorbing another heavyweight in Asian trade would allow China to boost its trade standing and further rival Japanese domination. However, to gain these benefits, any unification would have to occur peacefully and in such a way as not to disturb in any way the Taiwanese economic structure. Any hint of Communist domination of the Taiwanese economy could well cause an instant crash, with disastrous consequences.

Understanding this, China has been making very strong and repeated pleas to the Taiwanese such as the "One Country, Two Systems" formula, guaranteeing its form of economic policy, and has offered Taiwanese dominated internal politics. Further, it has allowed for a Taiwanese army to help maintain order in the region, thereby offering complete "autonomy" within the greater Chinese state. After all, both factions, China asserts, had agreed to the Shanghai Communiqué which stated that Taiwan and China were one whole country. Such guarantees would completely integrate the Taiwanese economy as a quick and clean transition towards a whole China.

---

13.   Braudy, 2003. p. 528.

14.   Ash, 1993. December. p. 712.

However, if things were to be that beneficial to the Taiwanese, there would be no further cause for conflict. Taiwan has seen what has occurred in Hong Kong in the name of the "One Country, Two Systems" policy, a policy that only promises 50 years of uninterrupted interference in economics and politics. Hong Kong, rather than see 50 years of its own economic system undisturbed is beginning to show evidence of Communist domination just 10 years into the programme. Internal autonomy was compromised by rigged elections, where many of its candidates were not even allowed to run for their prospective posts. Such overt subversion of the agreement between the Chinese and the British regarding the changing hands of Hong Kong is a possible indicator to what could happen to Taiwan. And this time there would be no foreign power backing the autonomy and institutions of the subject to be annexed. The US is aware of this and makes it clearly known that if there is a conflict, it will fight for Taiwanese sovereignty. The US could ultimately win this conflict, but it knows that from proximity alone Taiwan would pay a horrible price for war.

The Chinese economy would suffer not just from the loss of Taiwan as an active trading partner (internal or external), it would also suffer due to the immense transition that must be made from civilian to wartime economy, then back to civilian again. Money, not politics is the only factor that can play an active part in Chinese affairs, as has been shown by Chinese "Special Administrative Regions (SAR)", and money does not show a favourable outcome to any open conflict between China and Taiwan, with or without US intervention. Thus, the *status quo* will be maintained not as the most favourable solution for the people, but rather the most favourable solution for the economy.[15]

Regarding foreign affairs, China understands its current position in East Asian and world affairs. As the lone Communist state of any economic functionality, China is burdened as being viewed as hostile in

15. (Gabriella Montinola, 1996). *Federalism, Chinese Style: The Political Basis for Economic Success*. She states that increased political power within the SARs and the new autonomy that is presented by Hong Kong and will be presented by Taiwan will make integration after 50 years difficult and politically unlikely for whichever government inherits the situation. Rather, she proposes a Chinese federalist system that would alleviate much of the stress between the capitalist and communist regions of China.

any negotiations due to the system of its government. Further, China's offences against humanity continue to reduce its potential for world prestige. The US still enforces its arms embargo against the country that was instituted following Tiananmen Square. Perception is now the dominating factor to a country's influence in world affairs, no longer size of military. Perception is exactly where China consistently falters. It is imperative that it cleans up its human rights record, and, unfortunately for the Chinese Communist Party, that means permitting some level of direct democracy. Such an act would knowingly subvert the domination of the party, and is not likely to occur easily or in the foreseeable future. This fact alone keeps China influence on non-economic world affairs at a minimum. Only recently and after the administration of Deng Xiaoping has China made a significant attempt to enter the world community. No longer assuming the role of a world power without the responsibilities whereof, China participates on many international initiatives, such as the ending of border disputes between former parts of the Soviet Union, normalising relations with many countries within and without Asia, and trying to resolve its border feud with India.[16]

The US is aware of this isolation and attempt at rebirth, yet is also just as aware of its reliance on China for economic prosperity. In addition, it is aware that much of China's world participation is to create a barrier between the US and the countries in Asia it wishes to influence. While this means that the US will continue to negotiate with China, it does not mean that relations between the two countries are anything but cool at present. The spat over the USS Kitty Hawk's docking in Hong Kong (2007) was one example of the degree of fist waving and propagandist wars between the US and China. All this is not authentic hatred, but simply a conduit through which rage can be vented, understanding that war cannot occur in any degree between these two countries.[17] China is a nation at a crossroads. Formerly an isolationist, war-mongering nation concerned only with its own internal prosperity and revolution, China is beginning to emerge as an active and prosperous trading power. With an accelerating economy aided by unprecedented growth, China presents a new and challenging rival to US world leadership. While war is unlikely, the new

16.   Fravel, 2003. November-December.
17.   Fravel, 2003. November-December.

rivalry presents a favourable outcome in the form of active and accelerated scientific advancement and economic mutual reliance. While the future might not hold consistent sunny relations between these two powers, it does present an opportunity for these two nations to advance into the future in a spirit of accommodation and cooperation.

4 | Outlook for the Future

US-India *versus* US-China

Shared ideological perceptions help in accommodating each other's concerns within the framework of a democratic polity and make it easier for India and the US work together. This is not the case between the US and China which have radically different political systems, and hence approaches towards human rights issues, civil liberties and religious freedoms are widely divergent. The Tiananmen incidents of 1989 brought these differences into even sharper focus and the reverberations are felt to this day. The arms embargo by the US and EU that followed in the wake of 1989 is still in place. Contrast this with the "Global Democracy Initiative" that India and the US are actively engaged in or the Warsaw-based "Community of Democracies" initiative in which India, along with the US is a Convener. According to the US State Department, "The Community of Democracies initiative aims to forge international consensus among countries committed to the democratic path on ways they can better work together to support and deepen democracy where it exists, and to defend it where threatened." The Warsaw Declaration (2000) commits member nations "to respect and uphold...core democratic principles and practices" including, among others, free and fair elections, freedom of speech and expression, equal access to education, rule of law, and freedom of peaceful assembly. Similarly the US-India Global Democracy Initiative underscores the two nations' fundamental commitment to democracy as they believe they have an obligation to the global community to strengthen values, ideals and practices of freedom, pluralism, and rule of law. With their own respective solid democratic traditions and institutions, India and the US agreed to assist other societies in transition seeking to become more open and democratic. They recognise democracy as a universal aspiration that transcends social, cultural and religious boundaries. In terms of this Initiative, both countries have contributed US$10 million each to the UN

Democracy Fund. A virtual Coordination and Information Centre has been set up to share best practices on democracy, identify opportunities for joint support, and highlight capacity-building training programmes. Training courses are organised under this initiative in both the US and India.

According to the US Secretary of State, Condoleezza Rice, in the 21st century, greatness is increasingly defined by the technological and economic development that flows naturally in open and free societies. While technological and economic development is rapidly taking place both in China as well as in India, the fact is that India is a completely open, free and robustly democratic society, unlike China certainly is not. As a result, the US is much more comfortable in dealing with the technological and economic development in India, which is never perceived as a threat, as compared to that taking place in China which could assume a threatening posture, given the lack of transparency. Referring to India, the US Secretary of State further said: "This democratic nation promises to become a global power and an ally in shaping an international order rooted in freedom and the rule of law." Elaborating further, she added that Indians "realise their stake in a democratic, secure and open international order—and their commensurate responsibilities for strengthening it and defending it against the major transnational challenges of our era". Since this statement was made in the context of President Bush having expressed support for a reasonable expansion of the UN Security Council, it could be reasonably interpreted as an indication that if not soon, then at some stage in the foreseeable future, the US would be open to support India's permanent membership in the UN Security Council. This contrasts with an emergent China which is worried about conceding strategic space, or even sharing it with another Asian power. The US, on the other hand, is not; in fact, if anything the US would perhaps prefer to see another Asian power in the UN Security Council as is evident from her long-standing support for Japan's case—a scenario that China bitterly opposes and would perhaps never allow to happen. But there are deep-seated historical reasons for that antagonism for China to oppose Japan's membership. The same cannot be said of India, and given the demographic factor, not something that China can hold out on for all time to come. After all it is exactly the same reason for China being a permanent member of the UN Security Council. Whether it be the size of the population, or the size of the economy, or even the possession of nuclear weapons, there is no valid reason for China to be there but not India. And how long can one-fifth of humanity simply be ignored and left out of a key global decision-making body such as the UN Security Council?

Unlike the intractable Taiwan issue, the dangerously skewed trade imbalance, the question of currency adjustment/revaluation, or the frightening quantum of expenditure on defence which bedevil the US-China relationship, and will continue to do so in the future for lack of simple solutions, India and the US have no fundamental differences in the bilateral relationship today. Furthermore, policy differences during the Cold War apart, the US and India have never been in a situation of eyeball-to-eyeball confrontation with their armies as, for example, the US and China have been during the Korean War when the so-called "Chinese Peoples' Volunteers" (the PLA in different uniform, if that!) faced American soldiers on the battlefield across the Yalu River. Even though the US Seventh Fleet sailed into the Bay of Bengal in 1971, during the Bangladesh crisis between India and Pakistan, there was never any engagement, nor was a single shot fired. Indeed no US naval vessel entered India's territorial waters at the time.

Lately, China has been increasingly concerned at the growing US presence in central Asia. What started out as a US-led operation in Afghanistan in the wake of 9/11 to flush out Islamic militants, has since then morphed into a deeper engagement in central Asia with military bases in a number of countries. For Russia, this was her national backyard till the collapse of the Soviet Union in 1991 and therefore an area she still regards as falling within her legitimate sphere of influence and where she is reluctant to see growing US presence. China, equally keen to keep the US out of this region which she regards as her extended backyard and potential source for energy (oil and gas), has found common cause with the Russians to set up the Shanghai Cooperation Organisation (SCO) whose membership extends to several central Asian nations. India, on the other hand, as victim of Islamic militancy at home, does not oppose US presence in central Asia and was in fact the first country in Asia to offer US "unconditional" help after 9/11. Given the well-known strong linkages between the Taliban and Pakistan-based anti-India terrorist formations like the Lashkar-e-Taiba and the Jaish-e-Muhammad, the US and India share a common interest in ending the ongoing cross-border terrorism on the two respective fronts—the Durand Line to the west and the Line of Control to the east. To quote Sreeram Chaulia:[1]

> Islamic fundamentalism is a new factor motivating great powers to seek leverage in Central Asia. The anti-Soviet *jihad* of the 1980s unleashed a powerful tool of political mobilisation based on *jihad*. From Afghanistan, the virus of violent Islamism spread to the Uzbeks, Tajiks, Kazakhs, Kyrgyzs and Turkmens, turning the entire area into a nursery for global terrorism. All the four major contenders in Central Asia—the US, Russia, China and India—have a direct interest in managing the threat of Islamism emanating from the 'stans'.
>
> India's struggle for gaining a foothold in Central Asia rests on two legs—Afghanistan and Tajikistan. In the former, India has an abiding interest in neutralising the Taliban-Al Qaeda duo. The direct links between the Taliban and Pakistan-based anti-India terrorist formations like the Lashkar-e-Taiba and the Jaish-e-Muhammad imply that India can never be secure until *jihadis* from Central Asia are silenced.

India has a fragile toe-hold in Central Asia through a field hospital in Farkhor and an airbase in Ayni, Tajikistan, to help Afghanistan's Northern Alliance fight the Taliban. The US is quite comfortable with this because of Pakistan's recent propensity to enter into "deals" with the Taliban. These "deals" actually started under Musharraf under which the Taliban were free to do what they wanted inside Afghanistan as long as they did not take Pakistani prisoners or create any trouble inside Pakistani territory. It would be recalled that in 2006 after one such deal authorised by Musharraf, the attacks on NATO coalition troops increased substantially, and a number of Indian civilians working on civil reconstruction projects in Afghanistan were kidnapped. So much for the billions of dollars given as aid to Pakistan to fight the Taliban.

Of course, equally pertinent is the fact that while there is a constant debate in the US media, press and other influential intellectual circles on whether China's rise will be peaceful, nobody in the same circles ever asks the corresponding question of whether India's rise will be peaceful? Why is it always assumed that India's rise cannot be anything but peaceful. This is a question worth pondering over

The Rise of China *versus* the Rise of India

The close of the 20th Century witnessed unprecedented economic growth

---

1. A researcher on international affairs at the Maxwell School of Citizenship in Syracuse, New York.

in both India and China that has continued unabated into the early years of the 21st Century. China recorded near double-digit growth over most of this period, with India hovering around the same region but never quite matching China's growth levels. The onset of worldwide energy and food crises, the global fallout arising out of the US subprime mortgage meltdown and, in China's case the massive natural disasters (in the form of both earthquakes and floods) in 2008 threaten to bring down these high growth rates somewhat, albeit without substantially altering the basic architecture of growth and development. Both nations emerged from the relative chaos of earlier years to create a stable government and strong economy, and have subsequently emerged as leaders in both the Asian and world communities. What is especially interesting about the comparative growth patterns of India and China, however, is the dichotomy in the interpretation of that rise by other fellow Asian countries and the world in general, but by the US in particular. While we see lusty cheering and optimism towards India, China is perceived with suspicion at best and a threat at worst.

Why is this? It cannot just be economics that motivates this divergence in attitudes towards China and India. Thus, one must look at what both these nations have that make them distinct from one another. Perhaps it is a combination of past legacies, history and the ideology of governance that the rise of one inspires awe, whereas the rise of the other inspires fear.

It is very difficult for the United States to deal on an even keel with a communist nation. What China does at present is irrelevant. It is historical premise that mars this relationship. Soon after the People's Republic was founded in 1949, its main export (unlike consumer goods today) was 'revolution'. Initially it was the 'Marxist-Leninist' type and later the 'Maoist' version, but with the same aim—to help these movements overthrow established governments and set up communist dictatorships in China's own mould, in the belief that the postwar world was ripe for 'class struggle' which would culminate in the victory of 'the working classes' and the establishment of the 'dictatorship of the proletariat'. Thus it supported communist guerrilla movements from SE Asia to Africa and, wherever possible, beyond. That was the reason for the birth of SEATO, a US-creation to checkmate China's attempts at exporting revolution to Southeast Asia through moral and material support to leftist insurgencies, such as for example the Moro National Liberation Front in the Philippines, the Khmer Rouge in Cambodia, the Pathet Lao in Laos and the Vietcong in Vietnam, besides many others. It was also the reason for US's prolonged involvement in Vietnam on the basis of the 'domino-theory', according to which Vietnam was China's gateway to (exporting communist revolutions in) Southeast Asia. This is in stark contrast to India's attempts, for example, in bringing about democratic change in her neighbourhood—from Nepal (where it consistently supported the democratic forces) to Bangladesh to the most recent, in Bhutan.

China's human rights record ever since its inception has been appalling; lives lost during disastrous experiments with rural communes, the 'thousand flowers movement' and 'the great leap forward', not to speak of the 'Great Proletarian Cultural Revolution' run into millions. Even after the reform era began under Deng Xiaoping (1976) the world saw what happened in Tiananmen in 1989. The world still keeps hearing about the treatment that is being meted out to supporters of democracy—termed 'dissidents' by China. Such a poor human rights record leaves a bad taste in the mouths of leaders worldwide. The fact that China has done remarkably little to remedy this reputation perhaps makes it all the more difficult to view her economic expansion favourably. To many in the US, especially after the demise of the Soviet Union, communism is just about as evil as terrorism, and cannot be dealt with. This, according to Vincent Cable and Peter Ferdinand in "China As an Economic Giant: Threat or Opportunity?", when coupled with the partially closed door China shows to western economic interests, makes China a nation few can idealise, and many must inevitably fear.[2] We as humans fear the unknown. There is much unknown about China by way of its people, its government (Cable and Ferdinand remind us that succession in China has been a historically murky affair), and its future.

But there must be other differences between these two nations to present such a stark contrast. Lee Kuan Yew of Singapore, itself an economic phenomenon, wrote in 2007 that the reason China is feared is because its government is not unstable at all. In fact, it is the directness and near single-mindedness of its government that makes China such

---

2. Cable, Vincent and Ferdinand, Peter. "China As an Economic Giant: Threat or Opportunity?" *International Affairs*, April 1994. p. 243-261.

a threat to the United States. China's one party Communist system is directly opposite India's current system, which Yew notes is built to sustain 10-20 parties, all of whom are often at odds with each other.[3] The fact that India can create what Yew refers to as its own "domestic obstruction" puts world nations at ease.[4] This is not a nation of one consciousness but one that values intellectual discourse much like the US. It is subject to disagreements, to mistakes, to misdirection but always equally to debate. China, however, not only does not seem to allow itself to present fallacies, but looks down upon other nations for not embracing their economic models. Edward Wong of the *New York Times* reports that China has condemned the United States for allowing its economy to remain stagnant, touting the Chinese system as the ideal economic model for the world to follow.[5] While, according to Wong, the United States too is guilty of touting its economic system while it displayed periods of growth, China can only worsen its position in the eyes of the United States by this action.[6]

In response to these assertions, the question must be asked as to whether the views of the United States and the world over towards China can be changed. Can we learn how not to hold a nation hostage for its history? The answer must lie in the elimination of one of the major reasons the world fears China. China must open itself up. We must see without a veil how China lives, how it works, and how it prospers. We must be safe in our belief that there are no hidden creepy dragons south of the Great Wall, and the only things that go bump in the night are our heads on our pillows. This leaves a path that China has not gone down in nearly a century, and which is almost entirely counter to the values of the Communist leaders of history: it must embrace the world as we embrace each other. China is no longer small. It is no longer weak. It is no longer at risk to foreign penetration and manipulation as it was during the days of the Boxer Rebellion. Today China is only vulnerable to isolation. Cable and Ferdinand remind us that China has understood that it cannot afford to remain isolated as Mao had wanted. It must open up, it must embrace

3. Yew, Lee Kuan. "India's Peaceful Rise." *Forbes*. December 24, 2007.

4. Ibid.

5. Wong, Edward. "Booming, China Faults U.S. Policy on the Economy ." *New York Times*. June 17, 2008.

6. Ibid.

the world and it must embrace the fact that the world is becoming global and for it to survive, it must join that burgeoning community.

But perhaps we must finally come to a rational reason as to the true difference between China and India. This difference comes from attitude and social organisation. While China and India show signs of impending economic transcendence, only China (albeit not its original intent) has allowed its social fabric to also embrace this new, cosmopolitan, attitude. While India struggles to bring its social foundations up to an acceptable modern standard, China sets new bars in fashion, architecture, sports, and culture, making it all the more difficult for India to catch up. Lee Kuan Yew advances the simple proposition that perhaps the major reason why India is supported more than China is simply because India is behind China and can potentially serve as leverage in the future.[7] It is a modern manifest of the old British method of dominating Continental Europe: back the smaller power in conflict against the larger, and the resulting tip in the scales will leave just you in the dominant position.

There is a turning point approaching in the future. The age of the United States as a sole superpower is rapidly coming to an end, and the United States must force itself to come to an understanding that it must rely on other nations to keep its place in the world. This is a difficult task as the United States itself was formerly an isolationist nation. However, what will define the coming era is the perception the United States holds now of the emerging economic powers. In return, the United States itself must rethink its mindset as the defender of democracy and the standard bearer of humanity. For the sake of all three nations, the past must be put aside for the sake of the future.

Leveraging Relationships

That said, it must be understood that there are clear limits to how much the US, China and India would be able to leverage their relationship with each other. India will not be able to play the US card against China, just as the US will not be able to play its India card against China. Of course this assumption precludes the possibility of China using its India card against the US or its US card against India. Be that as it may, the sheer size of the

---

7.   Yew, Lee Kuan. "India's Peaceful Rise." *Forbes*. December 24, 2007.

three nations—economic demographic, political and maybe military—will simply ensure a power equilibrium—assuming no major hiccups to the current pattern of economic growth. Two well respected practitioners of international relations, Karl Inderfurth and David Shambaugh who, writing on the emerging relationship between India, the US and China, said (2005):

> There are some geopolitical thinkers in each capital who seek to use improved bilateral relations against the third party. Some in Beijing and New Delhi see strengthened Sino-Indian ties as a constraint on American hegemony. Others in Washington and New Delhi are suspicious of China and seek to build US-India relations (particularly military ties) as a strategic counterweight to growing Chinese power.

The current close relationship between India and the US began in the last years of the Clinton Administration and the fact that it has received considerable boost under the Bush administration shows that it enjoys bipartisan support. But President Bush is on record as having stated that these improved ties have their own strategic logic and imperatives, and are not designed as any China containment strategy. This has contributed in no small measure to correcting the perception that had grown in India in the summer of 1998 (after Pokharan II) that the US was not above playing its China card against India, when Clinton made gratuitous references about working together with China to contain India's nuclear ambitions. A course correction followed soon afterwards with the initiation of the Strobe Talbott-Jaswant Singh dialogue that resulted in a better appreciation of India's security concerns by the US.

Prime Minister Manmohan Singh is similarly on record as having stressed that the current strengthening of India's relations with the US is not at the cost of India's relations with China or Russia. But, as his predecessor, PM Vajpayee said: Shared democratic values and political systems make US and India "natural allies".

Natural allies or not, Indo-US relations will not be immune to ups and downs (witness only the continued US reluctance to endorse India's membership of UNSC), but a shared ideology, free political systems, commitment to secularism, threat of terrorism, even a common language, plus the absence of any fundamental differences will ensure a future of continued growth in bilateral ties, with the Chinese threat providing, at best, an unstated, but unignorable, subtext.

On the other hand, the Taiwan issue, China's heavy defence spending and concomitant military buildup, advanced missile and space technology, economic issues including lack of respect for IPRs, ongoing human rights violations, curbing of press freedoms etc., will continue to bedevil ties with the US.

Summing up

The point that I am essentially making here is that while a 'leveraging' that will lead to any major 'tilt' is unlikely, the fundamental ideological consonance between India and the US, coupled with the absence of any 'Taiwan' type problem of principle, will keep India and the US closer in this triangular relationship, though not necessarily to the detriment of China—which will be careful to calibrate its relationship with India in such a manner as to prevent the relationship from developing too strong a tilt against itself.

Thus we may find, for example, instances of greater progress, and even accommodation, in the bilateral India-China border talks, if China perceives that India is 'getting too close for (its) comfort' to the US. China would be deeply concerned with any major shift in the balance of power in the region in view of an emerging Indo-US strategic and military partnership and will do everything to prevent it from happening.

China's perception of the Indo-US military partnership, and lately the deal on civil nuclear cooperation, is that it is aimed at counter-balancing it in the region. Some statements by senior US political leaders in the Administration and Congress lately have only reinforced this perception.

The US's main concern is to build an effective counterpoint to balance China's growing economic and military strength so that it does not threaten its own security. A strong and friendly India with shared democratic ideals neatly fits the bill. The US also does not want to see too close India-China relations that might affect its own interests and position in Asia.

Future Scenarios

A somewhat simplified, interactive conclusion based on three basic parameters—Politico-Military, Economic and Energy—has been attempted between US, India and China, with the following broad results:

Between India and China, there is likely to be continued rivalry on both the political stage and in the military arena. China will never cede strategic space to India either in Asia or (much less) in the world and will do everything possible to ensure that India is always relegated to a secondary or lower status in the Asian hierarchy. It will do so by maintaining, and indeed dramatically expanding, the existing vast military and economic superiority over India. Given her highly disciplined and monolithic national political structure *vis-à-vis* a India's noisy, rambunctious and argumentative democracy with an abundance of contradictory and often centripetal political forces, that should not be too difficult a task to achieve. Besides strengthening herself at home, China will work through carefully nurtured alliances in Asia, especially in India's immediate neighbourhood, to ensure that any ambitions to challenge China's supremacy are kept well in check. On the global arena, this will translate itself into making sure that India never becomes a permanent member of the UN Security Council, or indeed any worthwhile political body where she can even so much as ever think of challenging China's supremacy. Should India ever attempt to do so by leveraging her relationship with the US, there is always the vast border on which threats can be translated into action. For this reason, China will never "resolve" the border issue with India permanently. Some portion or other will always be kept "disputed", or an old issue resurrected (witness China's volte-face on Sikkim recently) so that it can always serve as a handy powder keg to "teach" India a "lesson" whenever necessary about her rightful place in the Asian, or global, political firmament.

On the economic front, between India and China, things will be different. China will be keen to exploit India's vast market whose existing middle class of 350 million odd is likely to double by the middle of this century according to well-informed international economic think-tanks. Other than her own, there will be no comparable market anywhere else in the world, and given China's propensity of always succeeding in having a trade balance overwhelmingly in her own favour, just imagine what kind of a hold that will give China in her economic relationship with India. It will be a replica of China's current trade imbalance with the US (and we know what a stranglehold that exercises in US-China economic relations) multiplied several times over. It is a trap that India will carefully need to guard against, seeing the sort of problems the US is facing *vis-à-vis* China on this front—from currency revaluation to measures at rectifying the grossly-skewed trade imbalance. Investment flows between India and China, at present heavily unidirectional, will need to be balanced in future. In sum, while there be need-based cooperation between India and China in the area of trade and investment, the sheer size of China's economy will ensure an overwhelming superiority in her favour over India. This will be a challenge for India's economic planners.

In the area of energy, there will be acute competition between India and China. Both are developing societies with high rates of growth with concomitant vast energy requirements to meet their goals of building their infrastructure. Both lack energy-efficient technologies and rely on energy-heavy industries for their development. India is the world's sixth largest energy consumer with oil imports accounting for two-thirds of India's oil consumption. China, on the other hand imports a third of its crude oil consumption, but has proven oil reserves stand at 18 billion barrels, compared to India's 5 billion barrels. The scramble is already on and has contributed to the recent rise in oil prices, and will only get worse. China is highly aggressive in its pursuit,[8] acquiring oil blocks for exploration and development right from Central Asia to Africa, and from SE Asia to Latin America. India has caught on and followed suit but is lagging way behind. Often when it is just on the verge of making a breakthrough, China steals it from under her very nose.[9] In this gold-rush like situation, there are no friendly competitors, as India has painfully realised after having been lulled India into complacency by China through an agreement under which they will cooperate in preventing a bid being upped on account of mutual competition. India will have to be very cautious and careful in protecting her interests in this key area of energy where China will always be a competitor.

Between the US and China there will be acute competition in the political and military spheres, especially given the unlikely possibility of

---

8.   India's ONGC has invested US$3.5 billion in overseas exploration since 2000, while China's CNPC has made corresponding investments of an estimated $40 billion.

9.   In October 2004, ONGC almost closed a deal in Angola to buy a block for $620 million but the Chinese evidently cut a deal with the Angolan government at the last minute by offering aid to the tune of US$2 billion for a variety of projects to Angola, compared to India's offer of US$200 million for developing railways.

Taiwan's reunification with the 'motherland' in the foreseeable future. Over the years, Taiwan has developed an identity of its own which is quite distinct from that which was imposed when Chiang Kai-shek and his rump KMT came ashore in 1949. Partly this is because the native Taiwanese, as distinct from the mainlanders who came with Chiang, have become assertive in civil society, commerce and politics and see themselves as co-equals if not superior to the 1949 immigrants from the mainland. It is their country, after all, they argue and their party, the DPP, even brought the island dangerously close to formal independence, were it not for some wiser counsels, and with higher stakes, across the Pacific. Taiwan has, in a sense, become a test of America's will to remain the predominant Pacific power, just as much as it remains the unfinished part of China's communist revolution dating back to 1949. To maintain its predominance as a Pacific power, the US will also maintain its alliances with Japan and South Korea in good standing so as to keep rival China in check. China's response to this will be to strengthen her military and nuclear muscle, including sophisticated offensive missile capability to at least effectively checkmate the US in the Pacific even if it cannot match its strength. This explains the phenomenally high levels of defence expenditure and the recent show of her capacity to destroy satellites in space. In other words, China may not be able to openly challenge US military might in the foreseeable future, but it could easily keep the US at bay and prevent it from , say for example, even contemplating a meaningful or determined action to defend Taiwan, if 'push' ever became 'shove'.

On the economic front, unless the US works out some drastic measures to rectify the trade imbalance and the heavy dependence on cheap Chinese consumer goods imports, the present situation will continue. Irrespective of mechanisms such as the "Strategic Economic Dialogue" the Chinese will not be in a hurry to revalue their currency for the simple reason that more expensive exports to the US (the biggest market) will mean less exports, and so less work in factories at home leading to higher unemployment and social unrest. So, just as much as the US consumer has got hooked to cheap Chinese imports, China has got hooked to the US market for the survival of its factories at home. This unavoidable vice-like embrace will infect the bilateral relationship with some fear and justified suspicion without either side being able to do very much about it.

On energy and the environment, there will be more rhetoric than action between China and the US. The US will press China on both, but being herself equally vulnerable on both counts, will hardly be able to press the issue home. This may even lead to working together to identify long-term strategies for tackling these highly important emerging concerns. Unlike India and China who will be scrambling for the same energy resources, the US will not be a direct competitor to China or India.

India and the US, on the other hand, will increasingly find themselves on the same side when it comes to critical strategic objectives such as fighting terrorism and fundamentalism, promoting democracy or ensuring global stability. Their shared political ideology, the commitment to secularism and human rights and closer political and military engagement will help fashion a close partnership rooted in common interests.

On the economic side, trade and investment, both ways, is set to enhance by leaps and bounds and will be more balanced without any danger of it getting heavily skewed one way or the other. The business communities in both countries feel comfortable in their relationships which are greatly enhanced by people-to-people linkages.

On energy, irrespective of the direction that the civilian nuclear agreement takes, there will be close cooperation because the US is conscious of India's vast energy requirements for development and has shown genuine understanding in helping her meet such needs.

These observations, based on the analyses in the foregoing chapters, are now summed up in the following three diagrammatic illustrations.

Likely Furture Scenarios

Likely Future Scenario – 1

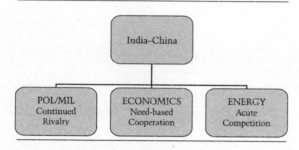

Likely Future Scenario – 2

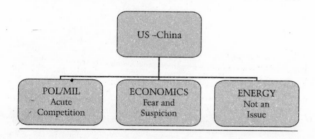

Likely Future Scenario – 3

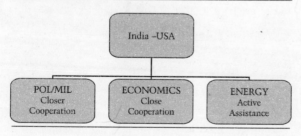

5 | Indo-US-China Relations under the Obama Administration

The Likely Scenario

In the twenty-first century, the emergence of India as strong, stable, democratic and outwardly looking global player with global interests has the potential to enhance the effectiveness of the international system and the security and well-being of all, in a positive sum game,....... "the real test of the relationship between the US and India will be how we work together on the great common challenges of our era—strengthening the global trade and investment system, addressing transnational threats like nuclear weapons proliferation, terrorism and pandemic disease, and meeting the urgent danger that is posed by climate change.

Jim Steinberg
US Deputy Secretary of State
26 March 2009

Just as this book is getting ready to go to print, and the Obama Administration approaches its first half year in office, there are indications that that the robust momentum in India-US relations generated during the Bush Administration, especially with the signing of the civilian nuclear cooperation deal (supported by both then Senators Obama and Hilary Clinton)—may perhaps not be sustained, at least in the short-term. The reasons for this are manifold and will be discussed here in some detail, but it will be argued that in the long-term there is far more consonance than dissonance in Indian and US interests on regional as well as global issues of strategic significance. In a similar vein, there is, in the immediate future perhaps a pressing need for the US to reach out to China in the short-term, especially in the light of the global economic meltdown, the situation in North Korea and the troubling 'AfPak' conundrum, in all of which China's help would be invaluable to the US. These issues are unlikely, though, to help sustain the bilateral relationship on a firm basis over a long-term timeframe. The reason is not far to seek. In the long-term, such is the nature of the beast that China can simply never change its stripes from being at least a strategic competitor, if not a strategic challenger, to become a strategic partner of the United States, periodic lofty and ritualistic declarations to the contrary notwithstanding.

Of course, India would not like to see any dilution in the upward trajectory of the ongoing relationship with a new Administration in Washington DC. The Congress-led UPA coalition under Dr. Manmohan Singh's premiership was highly enthusiastic about the growing ties with the US in its first term of office (2004-2009), and with same government re-elected with a thumping mandate in the recent (May 2009) elections, and no longer hampered by a communist albatross around its neck, would be able to continue friendly and cooperative relations with the US. It would be recalled that the Left parties walked out of the earlier coalition over the issue of the Indo-US nuclear deal, leaving the Government politically vulnerable and forcing it to fight for its survival in office by seeking help from other parties.[1] On the US side, it would not be difficult for the Obama Administration to see that a democratic India is the only island of stability in a turmoil-ridden neighbourhood in South Asia that includes the internally-imploding Talibanised Pakistan to the North, a civil war-ridden Sri Lanka to the south and a brutal military-junta led Myanmar to the East that is doing everything in its power to keep democratic forces (led by Aung San Suu Kyi) at bay with China's assistance and abetment. In this scenario, what really are America's options in this part of the world where it is itself heavily engaged in keeping Islamic fundamentalists at bay.

Notwithstanding these self-evident compulsions which should be driving the US policy in South Asia, the Obama Administration has not accorded India the rightful importance that it deserves. It does not require a great deal of political ingenuity to see that President Obama does not exactly share his predecessor's predilections towards India. Starting with strident rhetoric on outsourcing during his election campaign to the actual measures taken to cut H1B visas whose main beneficiaries are Indians, to leaving India out of all initial high-level contacts with foreign leaders and a patently lackluster meeting with the Indian premier on the sidelines of the G-20 Summit in London—all these are subtle indications of a dilution in the intrinsic quality of the bilateral relationship. On the other hand, one of Secretary of State Hilary Clinton's first ports of call has been Beijing, and

---

1. The unexpected but timely support came from Mulayam Singh's Samajwadi
     Party (SP).

President Obama, together with his senior advisors, has had a number of meaningful dialogues with the Chinese leadership since assuming office. Of course there is nothing like an overwhelmingly skewed trading relationship and control over a few trillion dollars in US securities and debt to grab American attention especially in the days of mounting unemployment, bank failures and a massive economic meltdown when China alone is capable of pulling large American chestnuts out of the fire. That is what rendered the zero in the G-20 economic summit in London somewhat superfluous, and everyone spoke only of the G-2 who mattered—China and the US—in that order !

Let us now examine the key issues in Indo-US relations and how each is likely to fare under the Obama administration

The Nuclear Issue

On the Indo-US civilian nuclear cooperation deal, President Obama was an early skeptic but eventually voted in favour of it in the Senate. He obviously saw the inherent advantages in maintaining the positive momentum of the bilateral relationship that the deal generated, going to the extent of assuring Prime Minister Manmohan Singh in a letter dated 23rd September 2008 that "if time runs out in the current Congress, I will resubmit the agreement next year as President." However, the same letter also spoke of the civil nuclear cooperation agreement opening "the door to greater collaboration with India on non-proliferation issues" with obvious implications for India. Assuring the Indian Prime Minister that he would work with the US Congress to ratify the CTBT, Obama went on to express the hope that "India will cooperate closely with the United States in these multilateral efforts", reminding him that "with the benefits of nuclear cooperation come real responsibilities and that should include steps to restrain nuclear weapons programs and pursuing effective disarmament when others do so." During a speech in Prague in April 2009, President Barack Obama again reiterated his intention to work on an early ratification of the CTBT by the US Congress

A tangible indication of what the US President had in mind came by way of Assistant Secretary of State for Verification, Compliance and Implementation, Rose Gottemoeller, who in her prepared statement for the NPT Preparatory Committee (Prepcom 2010) on 5 May 2009 named India, along with Pakistan, Israel and North Korea who needed to accede to the NPT, completely ignoring the exception that Washington sought and obtained for India at the International Atomic Energy Agency (IAEA) and Nuclear Suppliers Group (NSG) last year. This naturally has raised eyebrows in New Delhi. Not to leave any doubt, Ms. Gottemoeller went on to clarify that getting India to sign the non-proliferation treaty (NPT) "remains a fundamental objective of the United States." As India will see it, signing the NPT would be tantamount to India giving up its nuclear weapons, a goal that Washington has not insisted upon since the days of the Bush Administration. Following up on President Obama's speech in Prague (April 2009), Gottemoeller also stressed that once the US Congress is persuaded to ratify the CTBT, it would followed by an all-out diplomatic effort to bring on board the other states whose ratifications are required for the treaty to enter into force. That, of course, includes India. This introduces a hitherto dormant element in the Indo-US nuclear understanding which was predicated upon India's impeccable track record of non-proliferation, in keeping with which the July 2005 agreement implicitly recognised India's right to maintain non-civilian nuclear facilities that would be beyond the scope of international safeguards.

If this is indeed a conscious departure from the earlier US policies, it does not quite square up with the brimming optimism exuded by the future President Obama when he expressed the hope during his election campaign to be "working hand-in-hand with India to tap into the creativity and dynamism of our entrepreneurs, engineers and scientists" going so far as to say: "Imagine our two democracies in action: Indian laboratories and industry collaborating with American laboratories and industry to discover innovative solutions to today's energy problems. That is the kind of new partnership I would like to build with India as President."

The challenge confronting Indian diplomacy in this regard will, therefore, be to convince the US of India's security compulsions— sandwiched between a nuclear China and its client n-regime in Islamabad which is only paces away from n-weapons falling into the hands of terrorists, extremists and fundamentalists—something that the US is itself seriously alarmed about. These are the special considerations which render meaningless any possibility of India signing up to the NPT or CTBT and any ritualistic insistence by the US that runs counter to India's vital security interests will simply be ignored. India's democracy is as robust as that of the US, and any democratically-elected Indian government has to, and indeed will be, as mindful to the nation's key security interests as a democratically-elected US government. As fellow democracies, it should not be difficult to understand that. At a time when the Obama administration is deeply concerned about security in the region (AfPak plus neighbouring Iran), it should be making every effort to further strengthening the strategic partnership with a stable, democratic and strong India, not the other way round! With the electoral victory of the UPA and return of PM Manmohan Singh at the helm, it provides the Obama Administration with a unique opportunity it should seize advantage of. Letting it go would only be at its own peril.

The Issue of Outsourcing

Candidate Obama made specific mention during his election campaign that he would not allow American jobs to be exported abroad. Looked at objectively, jobs are exported more when American companies relocate their factories overseas (e.g. China) because of cheaper labour and other production costs than by simply having their 'back-office' operations (e.g. India) beyond their shores. That is a key difference in outsourcing to India compared to outsourcing to China. However, the important thing to remember is that neither takes place in a vacuum, so to say. It occurs because there is a clear 'demand' for a product or a service whose 'supply' or availability is cheaper outside the US than inside it. Thus, realistically, China has more to lose than India if President Obama is to adhere entirely to the letter and spirit of his campaign pledges. The truth of the matter is in a capitalist system, such decisions are made inside the boardrooms of a private company—almost exclusively on the basis of its perceived profitability (the 'bottom line')—and not in the Oval office of the US President. Of course, in theory, the President, with a lot of help from an obliging Congress, could conceivably enact laws to prevent the export of jobs overseas, except that it would militate against the very notion of 'free trade' so dearly espoused for so long by the US, besides the danger of running afoul of the WTO. Short of any drastic measures, measures such as tax breaks and other incentives may conceivably put on hold to at least slow the pace of outsourcing, but that too fails to take into account the resilience of countries like India and China to simply narrow their profit margins even further in order to retain the 'outsourced' entity—be it a factory, a back-office handling sales calls or sophisticated accounting and software development or a technical help desk. Some 400 out of the world's 500 largest companies are known currently to outsource work to India—and a large chunk of these are from the US. Soon enough they will discover that they may lose their competitive edge vis-à-vis their rivals if they just simply stop outsourcing their work. Let us not forget that the 'outsourced' worker in a foreign country does not make any demands on the parent US company in terms of leave, medical benefits, retirement benefits or social security, so that his 'overall' profitability is far higher than what appears on paper. Thus, putting a stoppage to outsourcing, in today's highly interconnected commercial world, is easier said in an election campaign than put into practice as state policy.

Just as the Obama Administration has put in place such measures as would favour those US companies who do not export or 'outsource' work overseas, a process of upgrading and re-engineering of software skills beyond repetitive operations is already in motion in India. Many are now working with or for US companies such as General Electric, Cisco Systems, Microsoft, Adobe, Motorola and Google who have set up engineering as well as R&D centres in India, taking advantage of not only cheap labour but also to put product development closer to fast growing markets. Today many Indian IT and outsourcing companies have developed advanced R&D capabilities which allow them to compete for high-end work for foreign MNCs. Clearly, helping to design and plan manufacturing of actual products is more profitable than running server farms or servicing corporate computer networks.

The upshot is that irrespective of incentives against outsourcing, or disincentives for outsourcing, commercial entities at both ends—the US and India—will work out a middle ground where it is profitable for both to work together. There are practical limits to what taxation or capping of skilled workers' (H1B) visas can achieve. After all is this not what capitalism is all about?

Terrorism and AfPak

It is by now an open secret that Ambassador Richard Holbrooke was originally to be named as President Obama's Special Envoy for South Asia, not just Afghanistan and Pakistan—that is to say including India. No sooner than India got wind of this, it was made known beyond any shadow of doubt to all concerned quarters that India saw itself as part of the solution, not part of the problem, which was the result of state sponsored terrorism by Pakistan—the most stark manifestation of which came by way of the ghastly terrorist attack on Mumbai on November 26, 2008 (commonly referred to as India's 26/11). It would appear that various South Asia specialists inside the Beltway also conveyed to the White House that this would be a highly retrograde step that could impact seriously on Indo-US bilateral relations which it had taken years since the Clinton Administration to assiduously build-up; and after all, India was the only stable and peaceful democracy in a sea of South Asian turmoil that extended from Afghanistan to Myanmar. By lumping stable, democratic India that was an even greater victim of *jihadi* terrorism than the US, with the likes of Afghanistan and Pakistan, would only hark back to the days of 'hyphenation' when the US could only see India through the Pak prism. Much effort had gone into painstakingly 'de-hyphenating' India and Pakistan from US policy considerations by the Clinton and (its successor) Bush administrations, all of which would simply be undone by naming Holbrooke as "Envoy for South Asia". It is not unlikely that both the Congressional India caucuses as well as the Indian American community would also have exerted their influence to make the Obama administration realise the perils and political cost of antagonising a perfectly friendly and democratic India by such an action. Ultimately, Ambassador Holbrooke was named as the special envoy for Pakistan and Afghanistan, and his journeys to those countries have included a stopover in India for consultations—not because India is part of the problem, but because India needs to be seen as part of the solution. This can be clearly seen in the sheer amount of civilian reconstruction work that India is involved in Afghanistan, often at considerable peril to her citizens working there, not to speak of other humanitarian, medical and HR assistance that India has unhesitatingly and generously extended to the government and people of Afghanistan. This only helps complement the US and its allies' efforts in Afghanistan, albeit on a strictly non-military platform.

Another area of concern that has lately arisen in India in this context is Obama's rather simplistic approach to the problem is a quick resolution of the Kashmir issue in order to free Pakistan to conduct the war on terrorism on its western borders with Afghanistan. If this implies rewarding Pakistan for its two-decade old ISI-sponsored terrorism in Kashmir in return for Pakistan's solid support to the US in Afghanistan, it is tantamount to India being forced to take the US's chestnuts out of the fire by burning its own hand and will therefore not be acceptable to India; indeed it may well set back an otherwise growing relationship. In recent years, even if reluctantly, the US has begun to recognise Pakistan's less-than-robust confrontation of the Taliban in spite of being generously funded by the American taxpayer for the task. The excuse of 'rogue elements' within the ISI can only be stretched up to a point; ultimately it is the responsibility of the Pakistani state to rein in these rogue elements if it lays claim to the dubious title of being America's 'major non-Nato ally'. Given this scenario, it would be unwise for the Obama White House to link a resolution of the Kashmir issue with the core of issue of eliminating the Taliban, and their al-Qaeda benefactors, in Afghanistan. In any case, for many years the US has now accepted the Simla Agreement as the basis for resolving the issue bilaterally between India and Pakistan, and endorsed the progress made lately by both countries in that direction. It would be better to keep nudging Pakistan in that direction rather than trying to reward it by interfering in the Kashmir issue when both countries are committed to resolve it bilaterally in terms of the Simla Agreement. The latest (26/11) terrorist attacks in Mumbai had nothing to do with Kashmir, else Americans, British and Jews would not have been singled out for killing. The Obama administration needs to understand that so long as non-State actors—as 'rogue elements' in the ISI are euphemistically called, are playing the political field in Pakistan, no effort at subduing the Taliban with Pakistan's help is realistically possible. It would be patently unwise for the incoming administration to reverse the 'dehyphenation' of the India-Pakistan equation that has finally taken shape in US policy after well over a decade since the end of the Cold War. To quote a seasoned Indian political commentator, "If India's national neuralgia over Kashmir is reignited under an Obama administration, America will risk losing all the recent gains in its relationship with India under President George W. Bush" and warned against Obama buying into the Pakistan Army's old argument that it cannot fight on two fronts—on the east with India and on the west against the Taliban and al-Qaeda.

Another rather simplistic notion also appears to be permeating in some foreign policy echelons in the Obama administration that both India and Pakistan are today facing a common threat from Islamic terrorists. While this may superficially appear to be so, nothing could be farther from the truth. It is tantamount to equating the terrorist with the victim of terrorism, and conveniently overlooks the fact that the very terrorists who are wreaking havoc in India (not only in Kashmir but as far away as Mumbai) are the creation of Pakistan's own ISI who cultivated and armed them for decades now, as part of an abiding policy to "bleed India with a thousand cuts." As often happens, these same terrorists are turning against the Pakistani state itself, but their ability to do so is only because of the continued support they enjoy from within sections of the ISI. Quite recently, the chairman of the US Joint Chiefs of Staff, Admiral Mike Mullen confirmed that elements of the ISI maintain links with extremists on Pakistan's borders with both Afghanistan and India. The New York Times recently pointed out that ISI support to Taliban commanders extends to "money, military supplies and strategic planning guidance." That President Obama has seen through this game is evident from his remark on 29 April 2009 "that the obsession with India as the mortal threat to Pakistan has been misguided, and that their biggest threat right now comes internally."

The China Factor

The fact that ever since assuming office, the Obama Administration has accorded a much higher priority to China, as compared to India, is all too evident. Partly, as has been pointed out earlier, it stems from the US-led global economic meltdown in which almost the only country that can single-handedly help the US out is China, what with its US$3 trillion in Foreign Exchange reserves and its being the largest holder of US securities. This, in turn, has largely resulted from the enormously skewed trading relationship that exists between China and the US. Earlier, the

US often accused China of deliberately undervaluing the Yuan which led to this enormous trade imbalance. Of late, the US has stopped doing that because a stage has been reached where these accusations have become counter-productive and, in any case, there is precious little that the US can do about it. If the west successfully hooked China on opium in the 19th Century, this is the closest that the Chinese have come to avenging that—by having got western, and especially, US consumers hooked to cheap Chinese manufactures. It is now a situation of 'no return'. Indeed, the US now scrupulously avoids even criticising China's human rights record, lest it hurts that country's sensitivities. There are indications that the Dalai Lama may perhaps not be welcomed with open arms into the Obama White House in the future. Meanwhile, China now brazenly intercepts US vessels in the South China Sea and elsewhere, eliciting only the mildest of protests from Washington. In the UN, it stridently supports repressive regimes, and vis-à-vis North Korea, it has let it be known that it will play the field on its own, not the US' terms. Sensing this change of attitude in Washington the astute leadership of Taiwan, well-versed in the art of tightrope walking, is becoming more focused now on finding avenues of co-operation with the Mainland rather than talking about independence or some variant thereof. Despite voicing its intentions to push the 'Reset' button with Russia, Washington is finding it difficult to locate that button. China, however, discovered that button quite a while ago and with it the elevator of Sino-Russian relations is ascending higher and robustly so. More often than not, it is at the expense of the US, for example in Central Asia, where both countries are cooperating feverishly to keep the Americans out.

Irrespective of the amount of strategic space that the US is willing to cede to China, or China is able to garner for itself in the evolving global scenario, the US will have to look out for stable strategic partners sooner rather than later. Going by experience of the recent past, US administrations have tended to start out with a Chinese honeymoon and ended with an Indian honeymoon. It happened with both the Clinton and Bush Jr. administrations and may well happen again. As for the present, it is clear that the Asian paradigm in Washington has undergone a major change—to quote former US Ambassador to India, Robert Blackwill: "China today appears, at least to me, to be on a substantially higher plane in US diplomacy than India which seems to have been downgraded in Administration strategic calculations", adding that the core strategic principle for the development of Indo-US relations under the Bush Administration "centered on the idea that the United States and India in the decades ahead both had enormous equities in promoting responsible international policies on the part of China and that deep US-India bilateral cooperation in that respect was in the vital national interests of both countries. It was with this strategic paradigm in mind that the Bush Administration treated India with at least as much importance as China."[2]

Some analyst have argued that unlike the Obama White House, the Bush Administration based its fundamental transformation of US-India relations on the core strategic principle of democratic India as a key factor in balancing the rise of communist China, with or without the possible subtext of "containing" China. The same analysts cite the successful conclusion of the Indo-US civilian nuclear cooperation agreement as convincing proof of that principle as it was a major, and unprecedented, concession to a non-NPT signatory. Whether or not China was indeed the 800 pound gorilla in the room that was responsible for the signing of the Agreement may be a moot point, but the fact that it witnessed a smooth passage through both the House and Senate says something of the covert apprehensions that must have weighed among lawmakers in both chambers.

For the record, it would also be recalled that unlike China, India refrained from hectoring the new President about the path he should adopt in dealing with it. In his very first telephone conversation with the President-elect Barack Obama, President Hu Jin-tao reminded him that "China and the United States should respect each other and accommodate each other's concerns, and appropriately settle sensitive issues between the two countries, particularly the Taiwan issue" (As quoted by the official news agency, Xinhua). Contrast this with the cordial words, and an unmistakable touch of personal warmth, of India's Prime Minister, Dr. Manmohan Singh whose congratulatory message on Obama's election victory said: "Your extraordinary journey to the White House will inspire

---

2. Speech by Robert D. Blackwill, former US envoy to India, in New Delhi on 5 May 2009.

people not only in your country but also around the world" and added that "the people of India and the United States are bound by their shared commitment to freedom, justice, pluralism, individual rights and democracy. These ideals provide a solid bedrock for friendship and strategic partnership between our two nations."

Speaking of the peoples' verdict in the world's largest democracy, US President Barack Obama said the election results, which resulted in the return of the ruling Congress Party with an enhanced numbers in parliament (May 2009)[3], had strengthened India's "vibrant democracy" and that the US would work to "enhance the warm partnership between our two countries." Generally speaking, there appears to an agreement among US think-tanks and South Asian experts that the return of a Congress-led government in India augurs well for the future of Indo-US ties. Looked at another way, it would not make geopolitical sense for the US not to nurture an already warm bilateral relationship with the only nation in this large swathe of a politically-unstable landmass that extends from Afghanistan in the west to Myanmar in the east, especially one with whom it shares a fundamental belief in democracy and human freedoms.

An Asia Society Report prepared by a specially-commissioned task force in January 2009 observed quite rightly that "we have at last reached a place where Indians and Americans can see our shared future together" and added that "what is significant is that the convergence of India and America rests just as much on shared principles as it does on shared interests. The Forbes magazine, in a May 2009 article went even further when it suggested "that if the Indian alliance is nurtured wisely by Washington, the U.S. could find itself with an ally of rare and enduring caliber."

Beyond the sheer atmospherics, these sentiments do underlie the shared ideals of the world's largest and the world's most powerful democracies because sooner or later, supporting a strong and resilient democratic India in an increasingly troubled Asian neighborhood and as a

3. After Pt. Jawaharlal Nehru, Manmohan Singh became the first prime minister to be re-elected in India after serving a full first term. With 201 seats in the 543-member lower house, the Congress Party secured the highest for any single party in a quarter of a century, thus giving it a clear and strong mandate to govern for the ensuing 5-year term (2009-2014).

strategic counterweight to an increasingly assertive, and sometimes even threatening, communist China will need to become a part of long-term US strategic thinking. No matter which way one looks at the emerging triangular relationship, the basic elements of this fundamental equation are unlikely to undergo any drastic change.

Timeline

INDIA-US RELATIONS

1947   **August 14/15:** India gains Independence from Great Britain, but partition of the subcontinent leads to the creation of the Muslim state of Pakistan.

   October: Pakistani-backed tribesmen invade Kashmir.

1948   The US first provides food assistance to India (PL-480 programme).

1949   **January:** UN-mandated ceasefire in Kashmir. A ceasefire line—now known as the Line of Control—was agreed.

1949   India adopts a constitution, making it a parliamentary democracy.

1950   Chinese People's Liberation Army (PLA) invades and occupies Tibet.

1952   First general election is held in India, showing India's commitment to democracy.

   First five-year plan is announced by Nehru, emphasising agricultural development.

1953   Vice-President Nixon visits India and Pakistan. Develops a more favourable opinion of Pakistan. India negotiates exchange of POWs between US/DPRK following the Korean War.

1954   Pakistan joins the US-sponsored South East Asia Treaty Organisation (SEATO), allowing the US military bases throughout the country.

1955   Bandung Conference establishes roots of NAM. Pakistan joins Baghdad Pact.

1956   India's Industrial Policy Resolution (1956) makes the state as primary developer of industry.

1957   The US and India have discussion on technological and economic cooperation.

1958   US and India hold discussions on defence. India claims it does not ever consider aggression against other countries.

1959   **Dec 9-14:** President Eisenhower visits India: "We who are free, and who prize our freedom above all other gifts of God and nature, must know each other better; trust each other more; support each other." India and the US reach agreement on educational cooperation. Pakistan joins CENTO.

1960   Air India begins flights to New York.

1961   NAM officially founded and holds its first conference in Belgrade. The US feels threatened as it weakens the traditional western alliance against communism.

            December: India liberates Goa, the remaining Portuguese colony on Indian soil. The US condemns the invasion, accusing Nehru of only adhering to the India's lofty principles of peace when it suits him. The US introduces bill in the UN to force Indian withdrawal, but it is shot down by the USSR.

1962   War breaks out between India and China in the Himalayas. India suffers a humiliating defeat. The US provides $80 million in military assistance late into conflict. Limited intelligence sharing with the US begins.

1963   The US and India reach an agreement to exchange civilian nuclear technology. Tarapur Atomic Power Station set up with the US help.

1963   **May:** The US Defense Secretary Robert McNamara, Gen. Maxwell Taylor, and President Kennedy meet to discuss the possible use of nuclear weapons against China in the event of another attack on India. Kennedy states "We should defend India, and therefore we will defend India."

1964   China develops and tests her nuclear bomb.

1965   **Sept:** Second Indo-Pakistan War over Kashmir. The US requests
        ceasefire in Indo-Pak War to evacuate the US citizens from
        Lahore. Pakistani abandonment of the US built Patton tanks
        indicates clear the US military aid to Pakistan. Pakistan
        also employed US built F-86 Jets and Sherman tanks, given
        specifically to defend against China.

1966   **January:** The USSR brokers peace—Tashkent Declaration. The
        US declines sale of military aircraft to India. The USSR accepts
        a similar deal.

1967   Stalin's daughter, on a visit to India, petitions for asylum to the
        US.

1968   India refuses to sign NPT because it is not applied equally to all
        countries.

1969   President Nixon visits India (July 31-August 1) and then
        Pakistan. Asks Pakistan to mediate between the US and China.

1970   **Dec.** Pakistan holds national elections. Sheikh Mujib wins.
        Civil war erupts. West Pakistan starts brutal crackdown over its
        Eastern half.

1971   **March-April:** Millions of refugees from East Pakistan seek
        shelter in India. Mukti Bahini, or Liberation Force of East
        Pakistan formed to fight Pak army from West.

        April: The US Consul General Arthur Blood sends a cable to
        the State Department outlining atrocities being committed by
        W. Pakistan in East Pakistan. The US takes no action.

        July: Kissinger tells Indian Ambassador if China takes a role,
        The US will be neutral.

        August: Indo-Soviet Treaty of Peace & Friendship signed. The
        US blasts treaty as breach of Non-Alignment. Indira Gandhi
        justifies by stating that relations will be pursued mutually with
        the US & the USSR.

        Nov: Indira Gandhi visits the US but fails to draw support.

        Dec.10: The US orders 7th Fleet into bay of Bengal, Soviet
        vessels trail shortly.

Dec.16: Pakistan defeated. 93,000 soldiers surrender to Indian Army in Dacca.

Kissinger on secret visit to China, takes off from Pakistan, which is acting as a mediator between the US and China.

1972   The US President Nixon on historic and momentous visit to China. Taiwan and Japan shocked.

1974   **May 18:** Pokhran I nuclear test. India calls it "PNE"or Peaceful Nuclear Explosion.

1975   Indira Gandhi declares emergency, in light of internal political crisis. Gerald Ford lifts embargo against certain weapon sales to India.

1976   The US discusses possible sales of nuclear technology to Pakistan.

1977   President Jimmy Carter sends warm greetings India, hoping for better relations.

1978   **Jan. 1-3:** President Carter visits India. Signs "Delhi Declaration" with PM Morarji Desai commiting to peace and democracy.

1979   India initially condemns Soviet invasion of Afghanistan, but soon modifies her stance.

1980   Deal to buy weaponry fails because the US refuses to allow production abroad.

1981   The US provides Pakistan with F-16 aircrafts; India promises to obtain matching weaponry.

1982   Indira Gandhi has successful visit to the US. Unlike Nixon, Reagan is cordial.

1983   Tarapur Deal (1963) expires; France replaces the US as supplier of uranium.

1984   India has a joint space flight with the USSR. The US agrees to expand technology transfers to India.

1985   SAARC established.

1986   The US signs six year, $4 billion aid package with Pakistan.

1987   India purchases Cray supercomputer from the US.

1988   Pepsi-Cola plant built in India. The US investment reaches
         $1 billion annually. The US agrees to provide fighter aircraft
         technologies to India.

1989   Fall of the Berlin Wall. Collapse of the Soviet Union.

         Beginning of the end the 'Cold War'.

1990   'Avoidance of Double Taxation' agreement signed between US
         and India.

1991   Liberalisation of Indian economy stirs private American
         investments in India.

         Industrial Policy Resolution (1991) removes many government
         restrictions.

         The US warplanes refuel in Bombay during the Gulf War.

1992   **March:** Kickleighter Proposals, Indo-US Naval steering
         committee meets.

1993   Congressional Caucus of India founded.

1995   First Framework for US-India Defence Relationship, to last 10
         years.

1996   SAFTA formed. Gujral Doctrine announced

1997   US/India sign Memorandum of Understanding over Space
         Cooperation.

1998   **May 11 & 13:** Pokhran II: India conducts underground n-tests.
         US intelligence fails to detect in advance. India cites threat from
         Pakistan and China as justification for going nuclear. China
         outraged. The US imposes economic sanctions but engages in
         high-level talks. Pakistan tests n-weapons two weeks later.

1999   Pakistan crosses LOC in Kargil sector of J&K but maintains
         they are only 'freedom fighters'. The US confronts Pakistan
         with intelligence that clearly points to the contrary and calls for
         withdrawal.

Dec: Indian Airlines flight IC 814 hijacked by Pakistani terrorists to Kandahar (Afghanistan).

2000   **March 20-25:** President Clinton Visits India, "Vision Statement" issued. India-US Joint Working Group on Counterterrorism founded.

Dec: Red Fort in New Delhi stormed by Lashkar-e-Taiba, a Pak-based terrorist outfit.

2001   **Sept.11:** Twin Towers terrorist attacks—India promises full support to the US. Shares intelligence with the US on Al-Qaeda operations in Pakistan and Afghanistan.

Dec: Indian Parliament in New Delhi attacked. India blames Pak-based terror outfits Lashkar-e-Taiba and Jaish-e-Mohammed.

2002   US/India hold discussions regarding join counter-terrorism efforts.

2003   The US led-invasion of Iraq is met with mixed Indian reactions, no troop support.

2004   **Sept:** Launch of Next Steps in Strategic Partnership (NSSP) by the US and India.

Senate India Caucus founded.

2005   **June:** Second 10-year "Framework for the US-India Defense Relationship".

July: Prime Minister Manmohan Singh visits the US.

Sept: Virtual Coordination and Information Center for Democracy established.

2006   **March 1-4:** President Bush Visits India. India and the US reach Bilateral Agreement on Civilian Nuclear energy cooperation.

2007   India's left parties are joined by the BJP-led NDA in opposing the Indo-US Civilian Nuclear Agreement, arguing that it limits India's sovereignty. Threat to withdraw support from coalition government of which the left parties are a part.

2008   **May:** Indian legislature is warned that time was running out to
            pass act during President Bush's term of office.

            July: Congress-led UPA Government decides to press ahead with
            the Indo-US Civilian Nuclear Agreement despite withdrawal of
            support by left parties.

Indian Prime Ministers since Independence (1947)

1   Pandit Nehru (Independence to May 27, 1964)   [INC]

2   Lal Bahadur Shastri (June 9, 1964 to January 11, 1966)   [INC]

3   Indira Gandhi (January 24, 1966 to March 24, 1977)   [INC]

4   Morarji Desai (March 24, 1977 to July 28, 1979)   [Janata Party]

5   Charan Singh (July 28, 1979 to January 14, 1980)   [Janata Party]

*   Indira Gandhi (January 14, 1980 to October 31, 1984)   [INC]

6   Rajiv Gandhi (October 31, 1984 to December 2, 1989)   [INC]

7   V.P. Singh (December 2, 1989 to November 10, 1990)   [Janata Dal]

8   Chandra Shekhar (November 10, 1990 to June 21, 1991) [Janata Dal]

9   P.V. Narasimha Rao (June 21, 1991 to May 16, 1996)   [INC]

10   H.D. Deve Gowda (June 1, 1996 to April 21, 1997)   [Janata Dal]

11   I.K. Gujral (April 21, 1997 to March 19, 1998)   [Janata Dal]

12   A.B. Vajpayee (March 19, 1998 to May 22, 2004)   [BJP]

13   Manmohan Singh (May 22, 2004 to Present)   [INC]

US Presidents Since 1947

1   Harry S. Truman (April 12, 1945 to January 20, 1953)   [D]
     VP: Alben Barkley (starting January 20, 1949)

2   Dwight D. Eisenhower (January 20, 1953 to January 20, 1961) [R]
     VP: Richard M. Nixon

3   John F. Kennedy (January 20, 1961 to November 22, 1963)   [R]
     VP: Lyndon B. Johnson

4   Lyndon B. Johnson (November 22, 1963 to January 20, 1969)   [D]
     VP: Hubert Humphrey (starting January 20, 1965)

5   Richard M. Nixon (January 20, 1969 to August 9, 1974)   [R]
     VP: Spiro Agnew (resigned on October 10, 1973)
     VP: Gerald Ford (starting December 6, 1973)

6.   Gerald Ford (August 9, 1974 to January 20, 1977)   [R]
     VP: Nelson Rockefeller (starting December 19, 1974)

7.   Jimmy Carter (January 20, 1977 to January 20, 1981)   [D]
     VP: Walter Mondale

8.   Ronald Reagan (January 20, 1981 to January 20, 1989)   [R]
     VP: George H. W. Bush

9.   George H. W. Bush (January 20, 1989 to January 20, 1993)   [R]
     VP: Dan Quayle

10. Bill Clinton (January 20, 1993 to January 20, 2001)   [D]
     VP: Al Gore

11. George W. Bush (January 20, 2001 to January 20, 2009)*   [R]
     VP: Dick Cheney

INDIA-CHINA RELATIONS

1947   **Aug15:** India gains Independence. The raging civil war in China between the Nationalists (KMT) and Communists (CCP) is approaching its final stage.

1949   **Oct1:** CCP is victorious in the Chinese civil war. KMT retreats to the island of Taiwan.

Peoples Republic of China is proclaimed with its capital in Peking (today's Beijing).

Dec 30: India becomes the second non-communist nation, after Burma, to accord diplomatic recognition the Peoples' Republic of China.

1950   **April 1:** Sardar K M Panikker appointed as the first Indian Ambassador to China.

Oct: Chinese troops cross the Sino-Tibetan boundary and move menacingly towards the Tibetan capital of Lhasa.

Nov: India refutes UN resolutions branding China as an aggressor in the Korean War, thereby directly opposing the US.

Dec: Nehru backs China's membership in the UN in a Parliamentary debate in New Delhi.

1951   **May:** China captures the Tibetan Governor of Chamdo and forces him to sign a "17-point Agreement" in Peking, conceding China's control over Tibet.

1954   **Apr 29:** Nehru and Zhou Enlai sign Sino-Indian Agreement on Trade and Intercourse between India and Tibet region of China in Beijing.

May 15: China and India sign Panchsheel, the Five Principles of Peaceful Co-existence:

1. Mutual respect for each other's territorial integrity and sovereignty;

2. Mutual non-aggression;

3. Mutual non-interference in each other's internal affairs;

4. Equality and mutual benefit, and

5. Peaceful coexistence.

June: Chinese Prime Minister, Zhou Enlai, visits India for the first time.

Sept: India expresses regret at the UN General Assembly resolution postponing discussion of the PRC's membership. Taiwan still recognised as China by the UN.

1955   **Feb:** President Rajendra Prasad says that China's claims over Taiwan is justified.

March: India objects to the inclusion of a portion of India's northern frontier on the official map of China, saying it infringes the spirit of Panchsheel.

April: Nehru and Zhou Enlai pledge to promote friendly ties at the Asian-African conference at Bandung (Zhou later accused Nehru's patronising attitude at this meeting).

1956 **Nov:** Zhou Enlai visits India for the second time on a goodwill tour.

1957 **Sept:** Indian Vice-President S. Radhakrishnan visits China.

1958 **Sept:** India officially objects to the inclusion of areas of Northern Assam and NEFA in a map in China Pictorial, an official Chinese publication.

1959 **Jan:** Premier Zhou Enlai expresses China's claim on about 40,000 square miles of Indian territory both in Ladakh and NEFA.

April: Dalai Lama escapes from Chinese repression in Tibet and seeks political asylum in India, which is readily granted, seriously ruffling feathers in Beijing.

Aug 13: China's increasingly offensive propaganda campaign for the "liberation" of Ladakh, Sikkim and Bhutan worries India.

Aug 25: PLA troops open fire on an Indian picket in eastern Ladakh killing one Indian soldier and overpower the Indian outpost at Longju, in North-eastern Ladakh.

Sept 7: Pt. Nehru tables the First White Paper on India-China relations comprising notes, memoranda and letters exchanged between the Governments of India and China between April 1954 and August 1959 in Parliament.

Sept 8: China refuses to accept the McMahon Line as demarcating the border between India and the Tibet region of China as it was imposed by a Imperial British India on a weak China. China further claims almost 50,000 square miles of Indian territory in Sikkim and Bhutan.

Oct 20: PLA troops fire on an Indian patrol in the Aksai Chin area of Ladakh, killing 9 soldiers and capturing 10.

1960   **April 19:** Meeting in New Delhi between Zhou Enlai and Nehru to address the boundary question ends in deadlock.

April 25: China refuses to acknowledge the Officials' Report— a detailed study of all historical documents, records, maps and other materials relevant to the boundary question—published by India as the basis for resolution of the boundary dispute.

June 3: PLA troops cross the Indian border in Shipki village in NEFA.

Oct 24: Indian Opposition leaders report 52 violations of the Indian air space by the Chinese troops in NEFA, Uttar Pradesh and Ladakh.

1961   **Feb:** China refuses to discuss the Sino-Bhutanese and Sino-Sikkimese boundary disputes and further occupies 12,000 square miles in the western sector of the Sino-Indian border.

July: Secretary General of India's External Affairs Ministry, R.K. Nehru visits China to prevent further deterioration of situation on border. Talks prove futile.

Oct-Nov: China starts aggressive border patrolling and establishes new military formations, which start moving into Indian territory. Frequent skirmishes along the border increasingly lead to serious clashes, with China moving into and holding large chunks of Indian territory.

Dec: India adopts a 'Forward Policy' to stem the advancing Chinese frontier line—involving essentially the setting up of posts to enable action to recover lost territory and block potential lines of further Chinese advance.

1962   **Jan 26:** PRC Government prevents Indian Embassy in Beijing from celebrating 'Republic Day'.

April: China issues ultimatum demanding the withdrawal of the Indian frontier personnel from the border posts.

June 2: China rejects India's demands to withdraw its forces from Indian territory.

June 3: Agreement on Trade and Intercourse between India and China lapses.

June 10: Indian and Chinese soldiers face off within a 100 yards of each other in the Galwan Valley in Ladakh and an armed clash is narrowly averted.

July 26: Both sides indicate willingness to hold discussions on the basis of the Officials' Report which China earlier disregarded, for the resolution of the boundary dispute.

Sept 20: PLA forces cross the McMahon Line in the Thagla region 2 miles east of Dhola in NEFA and open fire on an Indian checkpost.

Sept 29: PLA forces launch another intensified attack along the border in the North-east.

Oct 6: India again accuses China of intruding into Indian territory in the eastern sector and attacking Indian forces and pleads restraint.

Oct 20: China launches a massive multi-pronged attack all along the border from NEFA to Ladakh. India is caught unprepared for the sheer intensity of the attack and suffers heavy loss of men, material and territory.

Oct 24: After achieving all its military objectives, China proposes a three-point cease-fire formula—Both parties would respect the Line of Actual Control, the armed forces would withdraw 20km from this line and; talks between the prime-ministers of both countries to seek a friendly settlement.

Oct 26: In the face of heavy losses all along the border, India proclaims a state of national emergency. The next day Nehru rejects China's ceasefire proposal.

Nov 15: A massive Chinese attack on the eastern front, Tawang, Walong in the western sector overrun, Rezang La and the Chushul airport shelled.

Nov 18: Chinese troops capture Bomdila in the NEFA region.

Nov 21: China declares a unilateral ceasefire along the entire border and announces withdrawal of its troops to positions 20km behind the LAC.

Dec 8: China sends a note signed by Zhou Enlai to India reiterating the three-point ceasefire formula. Bereft of any military alternatives, India accepts the formula.

Dec 10: Colombo proposals endorsed.

(Six non-aligned nations—Egypt, Burma, Cambodia, Sri Lanka, Ghana and Indonesia met in Colombo and formulated these proposals. The proposals, negotiated between Zhou Enlai and Nehru, stipulated Chinese withdrawal of 20km from the traditional customary lines as claimed by China, without any corresponding withdrawal on the Indian side. In the east, the LAC recognised by both governments was to be treated as a ceasefire line, while the status quo would be maintained in the middle sector.)

1963   **March 2:** China and Pakistan sign a boundary settlement in Beijing between POK and Xinjiang. Pakistan ceded 5080 sq. km of territory in Pak-occupied Kashmir.

March 23: Official sources confirm massive induction of PLA troops into Tibet, raising concerns in New Delhi.

1964   **Oct 16:** China conducts its first successful atmospheric nuclear explosion in Lop Nor.

Dec 30: Reeling from victory, Zhou Enlai warns India that China had not relinquished its sovereignty over the 90,000 square km of territory south of McMahon Line.

1965   **March 26:** Sino-Pak boundary protocol involving territory in Jammu and Kashmir signed in Pakistan Occupied Kashmir between Chinese Premier Zhou Enlai and Pakistani President Ayub Khan.

April: China extends support to Pakistani aggression in India's Rann of Kutch (Gujarat State).

Aug 27: China accuses India of crossing the Sikkim-China boundary, thereby laying the groundwork to support Pakistan in the ensuing war against India (see below).

Sept: China supports Pakistan during the Indo-Pak conflict in Chhamb across the international border of J&K and officially accuses India of 'criminal aggression'.

Nov.: Chinese troops again intrude into north Sikkim and NEFA.

1966   **Jan:** China condemns the Tashkent Agreement between India and Pakistan as a product of joint US-Soviet plotting.

1969   **Jan:** India indicates its desire to conduct its relation with China on the principle of mutual respect of each other's sovereignty and territorial integrity and non-interference in internal affairs.

1971   **Oct 25:** The UN General Assembly votes to give China's seat in UN to the Government of PRC, expelling Nationalist China functioning as the 'Republic of China' from Taiwan.

Dec: India-China relations suffer a further setback following the creation of Bangladesh, as China keeps issuing stern warnings to India against interfering in Pakistan's 'internal affairs'.

1972   **July:** China vetoes an Indian sponsored resolution for the admitting Bangladesh to the UN.

1973   **April:** China accuses India of committing aggression on Sikkim on the pretext of disturbances.

1974   **May:** India conducts its Peaceful Nuclear Explosion (PNE) in the Pokharan Desert. China accuses India of nuclear blackmail by posing as a 'sub-super power'.

1975   **April:** China expresses strong condemnation and utmost indignation at the merger of Sikkim with the Indian Union.

1976   **April:** India and China decide to restore the level of diplomatic representation in both countries to the ambassadorial level after a 15-year diplomatic hiatus.

July: K. R. Narayanan (later President of India) is appointed as the India's Ambassador to the PRC.

Sept: Chen Chao Yuan is appointed as the Chinese Ambassador to India.

1979   Indian Foreign Minister Atal Behari Vajpayee visits China.

1981   **June:** Chinese Foreign Minister Huang Hua visits India to discuss establishment of an annual dialogue at the level of Vice-Ministers.

1986   Differences surface over the limits of the McMahon Line in Arunachal Pradesh's Sumdorung Chu area.

1988   Prime Minister Rajiv Gandhi visits China and sign agreement to set up a Joint Working Group on Boundary question and a Joint Group on Economic Relations, Trade, Science and Technology signed.

1991   **Dec:** Chinese Premier Li Peng visits India after 31 years, assures to resolve the boundary question through friendly consultations.

1993   **Sept:** PM Narasimha Rao visits China; Agreement reached on maintaining peace and tranquility along the LAC.

1994   Vice-President K.R. Narayanan visits China.

1996   **Nov:** Chinese President Jiang Zemin visits India, signs Agreement on Confidence Building Measures in the India-China Border Areas, including downsizing respective military forces along the LAC.

1998   **May 12&14:** India conducts n-tests. China initial reaction muted, but once she was cited as a cause for India going nuclear, condemns India strongly.

1998   **May 13:** PM Vajpayee's letter to US President Clinton is leaked to *NY Times*, in which he accused China of posing a "nuclear threat" to India. Defence Minister Fernandes reiterated the same. The Chinese government brushed aside the Indian accusations as "utterly groundless".

1999   **June:** External Affairs Minister Jaswant Singh visits China to reassure Chinese leaders that India perceived no threat from China.

        Nov 24: India and China hold detailed discussions in New Delhi on ways to settle their border row.

2000   **April:** India and China commemorate 50th anniversary of their diplomatic relations.

        May: Delegation from India's National Defence College arrives in China signalling resumption of military ties, suspended after India's nuclear tests. .

2001   **Jan 13:** India and China agree to counter terrorism together to maintain security and stability.

2002   **Jan:** Chinese Premier Zhu Rongji visits India. Six MoUs signed in New Delhi to enhance cooperation in S&T, outer space, tourism, phytosanitary measures and supply of hydrological data relating to the Brahmaputra river between India and China.

        Jan: The first Shanghai-Beijing-New Delhi direct passenger flight for boosting bilateral business ties and tourism announced by China.

        March 29: India and China agree in Beijing to quicken the pace of LAC delineation in order to resolve the vexatious border dispute within a reasonable time-frame.

        June: China permits Indian Ambassador, Shiv Shankar Menon to visit to Tibet.

2003   **June:** China, India reach *de facto* agreement over status of Tibet and Sikkim in landmark cross-border trade agreement.

2004   India and China propose opening up the Nathula and Jelepla Passes in Sikkim for cross-border trade.

2005   **April:** Chinese Premier Wen Jiabao visits India.

2006   India-China Friendship Year Celebrations.

2007   **Sept:** 11th Round of talks on the India-China boundary issue held in Beijing from between M.K. Narayanan, India's National Security Adviser, and Dai Bing-guo, the PRC Vice Foreign Minister.

        Oct: Congress President, Mrs. Sonia Gandhi visits China.

2008   **Jan:** Prime Minister Manmohan Singh visits China.

US-CHINA RELATIONS

1941-45   The US military forces join the Nationalist Chinese (KMT) government to fight the Japanese. The US aid is delivered primarily over 'the Hump' (Himalayas). President Roosevelt backs KMT leader Chiang Kai-Shek. The US public opinion strongly pro-KMT.

1944-47   The US Army Observer Group, known as the 'Dixie Group' stationed at Yan'an. Served as the only formal link between the US and Chinese Communists (CCP).

1945-46   WW-II ends. Chiang Kai-shek's KMT forces engage Communist PLA. The US support KMT with money and military supplies.

1949   **Oct 1:** Proclamation of the Peoples Republic of China in Beijing (Peking).

1950   **May:** PLA Forces defeat KMT forces for final time at the "Landing Operation on Hainan Island".

1950   **June:** Onset of the Korean War. US recognises Nationalist (KMT) Government in Taiwan and sends 7th Fleet into Taiwan Straits to block Communist invasion.

1950   **November:** Chinese forces make contact with the US-led UN forces in North Korea. The UN forces quickly overwhelmed.

1951   **January:** Chinese forces advance into South Korea, retaking Seoul and moving South.

1951-53   The UN forces repulse Chinese attacks, move North again. The UN generals decide to keep the "Kansas Line" as defensive position, prompting stalemate. Armistice signed in July 1953.

1954-55   First Taiwan Straits Crisis. Chinese batteries bombard Quemoy. Naval assault takes Yijiangshan Island, eradicating the garrison. The US passes Formosa Resolution promising defense of ROC and its outlying islands.

1955   **March:** The US Secretary of State Dulles threatens "new and powerful weapons of precision" against China in defence of the US interests in East Asia.

1955   **April:** Premier Zhou Enlai states that China does not want war with the US and is willing to negotiate with the US government.

1955   **August:** The US and China begin ambassadorial talks relating to the release of American POWs from the Korean War.

1957   **October:** The US Senator John F Kennedy states that new foreign policy towards China is necessary, stating that current policy too dependent on military-based strategy.

1958   **August:** Second Taiwan Strait Crisis. Bombardments from both sides of the Taiwan Straits. The US supplies ROC with weapons, aircraft, and munitions. Talks in Poland between Chinese and American ambassadors do not produce results, but crisis cools by October, with PRC announcing "even day rule" regarding Quemoy bombardments.

1959   **December:** Rockefeller report suggests the US revise foreign policy towards China, but admits Chinese still openly hostile towards the US.

1960   **June:** President Eisenhower declares while on a visit to Taiwan that the US will continue to back ROC, not the "warlike" Communist government. Reiterates that ROC is be the only legitimate voice of all China in the UN.

1961   **December:** The UN General Assembly rejects Soviet resolution to admit the PRC and expel ROC. This is the first ever formal discussion in the UN about appropriate Chinese representation in the world body.

1962   **February:** China warns the US that aggression towards North Vietnam and a mere military presence in South Vietnam threatens Chinese security and stability in South East Asia.

1962   **June:** Nationalist forces gather for possible invasion of Chinese mainland. The US privately assures China that it will not support any Nationalist attempt to invade the mainland, and publically declares that it will not tolerate any threat to Nationalist security of Taiwan.

1963   **August:** President Kennedy states that China might pose the greatest potential threat to the world since WW-II.

1963   **December:** State Department concludes that there is little likelihood of the Communist regime in China being overthrown. The US considers relations with China and Taiwan simultaneously.

1964   **May:** PRC Foreign Minister Chen Yi outlines conditions for better relations between the US and China-US withdrawal of support of Taiwan and formal recognition of the PRC.

1965   **March:** Richard Nixon (not yet President) describes the Vietnam war as a conflict between the PRC and the US as well. China says it will do all to expel US from the North Vietnam and liberate South Vietnam.

1965   **June:** The US announces end of non-military aid to Taiwan. Military aid uninterrupted.

1966   **July:** President Johnson publicly calls for mending of relationship between the US and the PRC.

1967   **May:** Chinese news reports that the US jets had been shot down the month before, and that the town of Ningming on the China/North Vietnam border had been bombed. The US denies bombing. Premier Zhou states that war between China and the US inevitable.

1968   **May:** United States invites Chinese reporters to cover 1968 Presidential election.

1969   **February:** Secret Kissinger memo advocates normalisation of the US relations with China.

1969   **May:** The US uses Pakistan as conduit to "feel out" possibility of expanded talks with China.

1969   **December:** The US calls for direct talks with Chinese. Lifts ban on non-military trade with the PRC.

1970   **February:** President Nixon announces to Congress that the US has made clear overtures to China to create a formal relationship.

1970   **November:** Zhou Enlai responds favourably to what he calls "US proposal for face-to-face talks" Recognises need for envoy to be high-level, but states talks will be limited to Taiwan only.

1971   **April:** The US Ping Pong team receives invitation to have an all-expense paid trip to China. Birth of "Ping-Pong Diplomacy".

1971   **May:** Zhou Enlai invites a high level envoy to discuss issues other than Taiwan.

1971   **June: The** US announces end of trade embargo with China.

1971   **September:** Nixon announces that the US will support PRC joining the UN Security Council, but opposes expulsion of the ROC.

1972   **February:** President Nixon pays an official visit to China.

1972   **November:** The US lifts travel ban on China—in existence since the Communist takeover.

1973   **May: The** US and Chinese Liaison Offices open in Beijing and Washington as unofficial embassies while formal diplomatic relations are being worked out.

1975   **August:** The US slows down process of normalisation of US/China relations, as USLO Head, George H.W. Bush foresees complications arising out of the US disownment of Taiwan. PRC enraged by decision.

1976   **June:** Democratic Presidential candidate Jimmy Carter promises full diplomatic recognition of China.

1977   **June:** In terms of normalisation with PRC, the US recognises necessity of severance of US/Taiwan relations, but on condition that PRC will not use military means in any atter :pt at re-unification.

1977   **December:** Joint US/PRC announcement that full diplomatic relations would commence on January 1st, 1978.

1978   **April:** Carter signs Taiwan Relations Act, which treats Taiwan as if it was an independent nation without formal diplomatic recognition. Such treatment includes arms deals, diplom? : immunity, and money lending.

1979   **March:** The US and PRC formally establish embassies in Beijing and Washington D.C.

1980   **August:** The PRC and the US boycott the Summer Olympics in Moscow due to the 1979 Soviet invasion of Afghanistan.

1982   **August: The** US/PRC release statement of the US commitment to slowly decrease arms sales to Taiwan in order to resolve the Taiwan question.

1982-89   Numerous diplomatic visits to the US and China by diplomats and heads of government from both nations.

1989   **June:** Tiananmen Square incident: The US and the free world are appalled. The US and Europe impose tough economic sanctions on China.

1996   The PRC conducts military exercises in the Taiwan Straits, creating the Third Crisis. Crisis ebbs and by the following year (See below).

1997   The PRC President Jiang Zemin visits the US—first Chinese HOS visit since 1985.

1999   The PRC Embassy in Belgrade bombed by NATO aircraft. The US claims intelligence error, bu_ China insists that attack was deliberate.

2001   **April:** The US EP-3 Reconnaissance aircraft collides with Chinese fighter plane over Hainan island. Following negotiations, crew returned to the US and aircraft released later.

2001   **Post 9-11:** China supports the US coalition efforts in Afghanistan and passes UNSCR 1373, a counter-terrorism measure in the UN.

2005   China passes Anti-Secession law asserting its right to respond swiftly and military if Taiwan were ever to declare independence.

2008   **January:** Chinese military confronts USS Kitty Hawk in the Taiwan Straits, causing a 28 hour standoff.

Appendices

Appendix 1

*Text of the PM Vajpayee's's Letter to US President Bill Clinton
After India's Nuclear Tests in May 1998*

Dear Mr President,

You would already be aware of the underground nuclear tests carried out in India. In this letter, I would like to explain the rationale for the tests.

I have been deeply concerned at the deteriorating security environment, specially the nuclear environment, faced by India for some years past. We have an overt nuclear weapon state on our borders, a state which committed armed aggression against India in 1962. Although our relations with that country have improved in the last decade or so, an atmosphere of distress persists mainly due to the unresolved border problem. To add to the distress that country has materially helped another neighbour of ours to become a covert nuclear weapons state. At the hands of this bitter neighbour we have suffered three aggressions in the last fifty years. And for the last ten years we have been the victim of unremitting terrorism and militancy sponsored by it in several parts of our country, specially Punjab and Jammu & Kashmir. Fortunately, the faith of the people in our democratic system as also their patriotism has enabled India to counter the activities of the terrorists and militants aided and abetted from abroad. The deteriorating security environment, specially the nuclear environment faced by India for some years past has forced us to undertake limited number of tests which pose no danger to any country which has no inimical intention towards India.

I urge you, Mr President, to show understanding towards India's security concerns.

India's commitment to participate in non-discriminatory and verifiable global disarmament measures is amply demonstrated by our adherence to the two conventions on biologial and chemical weapons. In particular we are ready to participate in the negotiations to be held in Geneva in the conference on disarmament for the conclusion of a fissile material cut-off treaty.

May 13, 1998
New Delhi

Appendix 2

India–US Relations: A Vision for the 21st Century
New Delhi, India, 21 March 2000

At the dawn of a new century, President Clinton and Prime Minister Vajpayee resolve to create a closer and qualitatively new relationship between the United States and India.

We are two of the world's largest democracies. We are nations forged from many traditions and faiths, proving year after year that diversity is our strength. From vastly different origins and experiences, we have come to the same conclusions: that freedom and democracy are the strongest bases for both peace and prosperity, and that they are universal aspirations, constrained neither by culture nor levels of economic development

There have been times in the past when our relationship drifted without a steady course. As we now look towards the future, we are convinced that it is time to chart a new and purposeful direction in our relationship.

Globalization is erasing boundaries and building networks between nations and peoples, economies and cultures. The world is increasingly coming together around the democratic ideals India and the United States have long championed and lived by.

Together, we represent a fifth of the world's people, more than a quarter of the world's economy. We have built creative, entrepreneurial societies. We are leaders in the information age. The currents of commerce and culture that link our societies run strong and deep. In many ways, the character of the 21st century world will depend on the success of our cooperation for peace, prosperity, democracy and freedom.

That presents us with an opportunity, but also a profound responsibility to work together. Our partnership of shared ideals leads us to seek a natural partnership of shared endeavors.

In the new century, India and the United States will be partners in peace, with a common interest in and complementary responsibility for ensuring regional and international security. We will engage in regular consultations on, and work together for, strategic stability in Asia and beyond. We will bolster joint efforts to counter terrorism and meet other challenges to regional peace. We will strengthen the international security system, including in the United Nations, and support the United Nations in its peacekeeping efforts. We acknowledge that tensions in South Asia can only be resolved by the nations of South Asia. India is committed to enhancing cooperation, peace and stability in the region.

India and the United States share a commitment to reducing and ultimately eliminating nuclear weapons, but we have not always agreed on how to reach this common goal. The United States believes India should forgo nuclear weapons. India believes that it needs to maintain a credible minimum nuclear deterrent in keeping with its own assessment of its security needs. Nonetheless, India and the US are prepared to work together to prevent the proliferation of nuclear weapons and their means of delivery. To this end, we will persist with and build upon the productive bilateral dialogue already underway.

We reaffirm our respective voluntary commitments to forgo further nuclear explosive tests. We will work together and with others for an early commencement of negotiations on a treaty to end the production of fissile materials for nuclear weapons. We have both shown strong commitments to export controls, and will continue to strengthen them. We will work together to prevent the spread of dangerous technologies. We are committed to build confidence and reduce the chances of miscalculation. We will pursue our security needs in a restrained and responsible manner, and will not engage in nuclear and missile arms races. We will seek to narrow our differences and increase mutual understanding on non-proliferation and security issues. This will help us to realize the full potential of Indo-U.S. relations and contribute significantly to regional and global security.

The true measure of our strength lies in the ability of our people to shape their destiny and to realize their aspirations for a better life. That is why the United States and India are and will be allies in the cause of democracy. We will share our experience in nurturing and strengthening democratic institutions the world over and fighting the challenge to democratic order from forces such as terrorism. We will cooperate with others to launch an international Community of Democracies this year.

The United States applauds India's success in opening its economy, its achievements in science and technology, its commitment to a new wave of economic expansion and reform, and its determination to bring the benefits of economic growth to all its people. Our nations pledge to reduce impediments to bilateral trade and investment and to expand commerce between us, especially in the emerging knowledge-based industries and high-technology areas.

We will work together to preserve stability and growth in the global economy as well. And we will join in an unrelenting battle against poverty in the world, so that the promise of a new economy is felt everywhere and no nation is left behind. That is among the fundamental challenges of our time. Opening trade and resisting protectionism are the best means for meeting it. We support an open, equitable and transparent rule-based multilateral trading system, and we will work together to strengthen it. We agree that developed countries should embrace policies that offer developing countries the opportunity to grow, because growth is the key to rising incomes and rising standards. At the same time, we share the conviction that human development also requires empowerment of people and availability of basic freedoms.

As leaders in the forefront of the new high-technology economy, we recognize that countries can achieve robust economic growth while protecting the environment and taking action to combat climate change. We will do our part to meet the global environmental challenges, including climate change and the impacts of air and water pollution on human health.

We also pledge a common effort to battle the infectious diseases that kill people and retard progress in so many countries. India is at the forefront of the global effort that has brought us to the threshold of the eradication of polio. With leadership, joint research, and application of modern science, we can and will do the same for the leading killers of our time, including AIDS, malaria and tuberculosis.

We are proud of the cooperation between Indians and Americans in advancing frontiers of knowledge. But even as we unravel the mysteries of time and space, we must continue to apply our knowledge to older challenges: eradicating human suffering, disease and poverty. In the past, our cooperation helped ease mass hunger in the world. In the future, it will focus as well on the development of clean energy, health, and education.

Our partnership is not an end in itself, but a means to all these ends. And it is reinforced by the ties of scholarship, commerce, and increasingly of kinship among our people. The industry, enterprise and cultural contributions of Americans of Indian heritage have enriched and enlivened both our societies.

Today, we pledge to deepen the Indian-American partnership in tangible ways, always seeking to reconcile our differences through dialogue and engagement, always seizing opportunities to advance the countless interests we have in common. As a first step, President Clinton has invited Prime Minister Vajpayee to visit Washington at a mutually convenient opportunity, and the Prime Minister has accepted that invitation. Henceforth, the President of the United States and the Prime Minister of India should meet regularly to institutionalize our dialogue. We have also agreed on and separately outlined an architecture of additional high-level consultations, and of joint working groups, across the broad spectrum of areas in which we are determined to institutionalise our enhanced cooperation. And we will encourage even stronger people-to-people ties.

For India and the United States, this is a day of new beginnings. We have before us for the first time in 50 years the possibility to realise the full potential of our relationship. We will work to seize that chance, for our benefit and all those with whom we share this increasingly interdependent world.

Atal Bihari Vajpayee   William Jefferson Clinton
Prime Minister of India   President of the United States of America

Done on March 21, 2000 at New Delhi

Appendix 3

A Shared Vision for the 21st Century of the People's Republic of China and the Republic of India, Beijing, China, 14 January 2008

H.E. Mr. Wen Jiabao, Premier of the State Council of the People's Republic of China and H.E. Dr. Manmohan Singh, Prime Minister of the Republic of India, meeting in Beijing on 14 January 2008, resolve to promote the building of a harmonious world of durable peace and common prosperity through developing the Strategic and Cooperative Partnership for Peace and Prosperity between the two countries.

China and India (hereinafter referred to as the "two sides") are the two largest developing nations on earth representing more than one-third of humanity. The two sides recognize that both China and India bear a significant historical responsibility to ensure comprehensive, balanced and sustainable economic and social development of the two countries and to promote peace and development in Asia and the world as a whole.

The two sides are convinced that it is time to look to the future in building a relationship of friendship and trust, based on equality, in which each is sensitive to the concerns and aspirations of the other. The two sides reiterate that China-India friendship and common development will have a positive influence on the future of the international system. China-India relations are not targeted at any country, nor will it affect their friendship with other countries.

The two sides believe that in the new century, Panchsheel, the Five Principles of Peaceful Co-existence, should continue to constitute the basic guiding principles for good relations between all countries and for creating the conditions for realising peace and progress of humankind. An international system founded on these principles will be fair, rational, equal and mutually beneficial, will promote durable peace and common prosperity, create equal opportunities and eliminate poverty and discrimination.

The two sides hold that the right of each country to choose its own path of social, economic and political development in which fundamental human rights and the rule of law are given their due place, should be respected. An international system founded in tolerance and respect for diversity will promote the cause of peace and reduce the use, or threat of use, of force. The two sides favour an open and inclusive international system and believe that drawing lines on the ground of ideologies and values, or on geographical criteria, is not conducive to peaceful and harmonious coexistence.

The two sides believe that the continuous democratization of international relations and multilateralism are an important objective in the new century. The central role of the United Nations in promoting international peace, security and development should be recognized and promoted. The two sides support comprehensive reform of the United Nations, including giving priority to increasing the representation of developing countries in the Security Council. The Indian side reiterates its aspirations for permanent membership of the UN Security Council. The Chinese side attaches great importance to India's position as a major developing country in international affairs. The Chinese side understands and supports India's aspirations to play a greater role in the United Nations, including in the Security Council.

The two sides support and encourage the processes of regional integration that provide mutually beneficial opportunities for growth, as an important feature of the emerging international economic system. The two sides positively view each others' participation in regional processes and agree to strengthen their coordination and consultation within regional cooperation mechanisms including the East Asia Summit, to explore together and with other countries a new architecture for closer regional cooperation in Asia, and to make joint efforts for further regional integration of Asia. The two sides will strengthen their coordination under the framework of Asia-Europe Meeting, and are committed to strengthening and deepening Asia-Europe comprehensive partnership.

The two sides take a positive view on each other's participation in sub-regional multilateral cooperation processes between like minded countries, including South Asian Association for Regional Cooperation, Bay of Bengal Initiative for Multi-Sectoral Technical and Economic Cooperation and Shanghai Cooperation Organization. The two sides hold that this does not affect either country's existing friendly relations or cooperation with other countries.

The two sides welcome the positive facets of economic globalization, and are ready to face and meet its challenges, and will work with other countries towards balanced and mutually beneficial economic globalization. The two sides believe that the establishment of an open, fair, equitable, transparent and rule-based multilateral trading system is the common aspiration of all countries. The two sides favour the early conclusion of the Doha Development Round, placing the issues that affect the poorest of the poor at its core. The two sides are determined to strengthen their coordination with other developing countries in order to secure their shared objectives.

The two sides are convinced that it is in the common interest of the international community to establish an international energy order that is fair, equitable, secure and stable, and to the benefit of the entire international community. The two sides are committed to making joint efforts to diversify the global energy mix and enhance the share of clean and renewable energy, so as to meet the energy requirements of all countries.

The two sides welcome the opportunity for their outstanding scientists to work together in the International Thermonuclear Experimental Reactor (ITER) project, which is of great potential significance in meeting the global energy challenge in an environmentally sustainable manner. As two countries with advanced scientific capabilities, the two sides pledge to promote bilateral cooperation in civil nuclear energy, consistent with their respective international commitments, which will contribute to energy security and to dealing with risks associated with climate change.

The two sides recognize the challenge that humankind faces from climate change. The two sides take the issue of climate change seriously and reiterate their readiness to join the international community in the efforts to address climate change. The two sides also stand ready to enhance technological cooperation between the two countries. The two sides welcome the outcome of the United Nations Framework Convention on Climate Change (UNFCCC) meeting in Bali in December 2007 and agree to work closely during the negotiation process laid out in the Bali Road Map for long term cooperative action under the Convention. The two sides emphasise the importance of addressing climate change in accordance with principles and provisions of the UNFCCC and its Kyoto Protocol, in particular the principle of common but differentiated responsibilities.

The two sides appeal to the international community to move forward the processes of multilateral arms control, disarmament and non-proliferation. Outer space is the common heritage of humankind. It is the responsibility of all space-faring nations to commit to the peaceful uses of outer space. The two sides express their categorical opposition to the weaponisation and arms race in outer space.

The two sides strongly condemn the scourge of terrorism in all its forms and manifestations, and in all regions of the world. The two sides pledge to work together and with the international community to strengthen the global framework against terrorism in a long-term, sustained and comprehensive manner.

The two sides believe that cultural and religious tolerance and dialogue between civilizations and peoples will contribute to overall peace and stability of our world. The two sides endorse all efforts to promote inter-civilizational and inter-faith dialogues.

The two sides believe that their bilateral relationship in this century will be of significant regional and global influence. The two sides will therefore continue to build their Strategic and Cooperative Partnership in a positive way. As major economies in their region, the two sides believe that the strong growth in their trade and economic relations is mutually beneficial, and welcome the conclusion of a Feasibility Study on a Regional Trading Arrangement (RTA) between the two countries. According to the report of the Feasibility Study, a China-India RTA will be mutually advantageous. Against the backdrop of accelerating regional economic integration in Asia, the two sides agree to explore the possibility of commencing discussions on a mutually beneficial and high-quality RTA that meets the common aspirations of both countries, and will also benefit the region.

The two sides will continuously promote confidence building measures through steadily enhanced contacts in the field of defence. The two sides therefore welcome the commencement of the China-India Defence Dialogue and express their satisfaction at the successful conclusion of the first joint anti-terrorism training between their armed forces in December 2007. The two sides also welcome their efforts to set an example on trans-border rivers by commencing cooperation since 2002. The Indian side highly appreciates the assistance extended by China on the provision of flood season hydrological data which has assisted India in ensuring the safety and security of its population in the regions along these rivers. The two sides agree that this has contributed positively to building mutual understanding and trust.

The two sides remain firmly committed to resolving outstanding differences, including on the boundary question, through peaceful negotiations, while ensuring that such differences are not allowed to affect the positive development of bilateral relations. The two sides reiterate their determination to seek a fair, reasonable and mutually acceptable solution to the boundary question and to build a boundary of peace and friendship on the basis of the Agreement on Political Parameters and Guiding Principles for the Settlement of the China-India Boundary Question concluded in April 2005. The Special Representatives shall complete at an early date the task of arriving at an agreed framework of settlement on the basis of this Agreement.

The Indian side recalls that India was among the first countries to recognize that there is one China and that its one China policy has remained unaltered. The Indian side states that it would continue to abide by its one China policy, and oppose any activity that is against the one China principle. The Chinese side expresses its appreciation for the Indian position.

The two sides recognize the responsibilities and obligations of the two countries to the international community. The two sides are determined to enhance mutual understanding and friendship between the peoples of China and India, for the betterment of both countries and to bring about a brighter future for humanity.

Index

A

Afghanistan 23, 25, 26, 37, 39, 40, 41, 101, 102, 132, 134, 149, 150

AfPak 115, 119, 121

Afro-Asian solidarity 50

agricultural research 45

Aksai Chin 53, 58, 63, 64, 68, 71, 138

   plateau 53

allies 15, 16, 90, 153

Al-Zawahiri, Ayman 40

Al-Qaeda 40, 134

American

   Constitution 17

   diplomacy 80, 90

Anti-Missile Defense System 81

Anti-Secession Act of 2005 85

apartheid 17

Arabian Sea 35

Armitage, Richard 40

arms embargo 80, 96, 99

Arunachal Pradesh 20, 53, 54, 56, 58, 59, 64, 66-68, 71, 143

ASEAN 65, 67

   ASEAN+3 67

B

Baghdad Pact 19, 129

Bahini, Mukti 22, 131

Bangladesh 21, 22, 55, 64, 101, 104, 142

barriers, non-tariff 25

Beijing 18, 22, 50-53, 55, 60, 61, 77, 78, 81, 84, 107, 136-139, 141, 144, 145, 148, 149, 155

   Beijing-Islamabad-Washington Axis 22

bilateral

   cooperation 41, 44, 156

   interaction 34

   relations/relationship 14, 18, 20, 28, 32, 42, 45, 47, 58-60, 68, 73, 81, 101, 107, 111, 157, 158

   trade 25, 29, 42, 62, 68, 153

BIMST-EC 65

biotechnology 33, 43

border

   issue 60, 66, 109

   problem 64, 68, 151

Britain 15, 16, 31, 49, 58

British 15, 35, 46, 49, 51-53, 58, 70, 95, 106, 138

   colonialism 15

Buddha 50

Burns, Nicholas 17

Bush, George 28, 34-36, 38, 41, 47, 48, 80, 81, 87, 100, 107

   administration 27, 107, 115, 118, 121, 125